AGRICULTURE AND THE GATT:
REWRITING THE RULES

POLICY ANALYSES IN INTERNATIONAL ECONOMICS   20

AGRICULTURE AND THE GATT: REWRITING THE RULES

Dale E. Hathaway

92-1369

INSTITUTE FOR INTERNATIONAL ECONOMICS
WASHINGTON, DC
SEPTEMBER 1987

Dale E. Hathaway, a Visiting Fellow at the Institute, is a partner in the Consultants International Group, Inc. He was formerly Under Secretary of Agriculture for International Affairs and Commodity Programs (1979–81); Assistant Secretary of Agriculture (1977–79); Director of the International Food Policy Research Institute (1975–77); and served twice as a senior staff member of the President's Council of Economic Advisers, 1955–56 and 1962–63. He was a faculty member in Agricultural Economics; Professor and Department Chairman, at Michigan State University (1948–72); President and Fellow of the American Agricultural Economics Association; and the winner of three national awards for published research. He has written three books and numerous articles and monographs on agricultural policy and trade issues.

The author acknowledges with thanks the invaluable assistance of Lana Hall and Janet E. Rasmussen in the development of the information and statistics in this study.　　　D.E.H.

INSTITUTE FOR INTERNATIONAL ECONOMICS
11 Dupont Circle, NW
Washington, DC 20036
(202)328-9000 Telex: 248329 CEIP Fax (202)328-5432

C. Fred Bergsten, *Director*
Ann L. Beasley, *Director of Publications*

The Institute for International Economics was created, and is principally funded, by the German Marshall Fund of the United States.

The views expressed in this publication are those of the authors. This publication is part of the overall program of the Institute, as endorsed by its Board of Directors, but does not necessarily reflect the views of individual members of the Board or the Advisory Committee.

Printed in the United States of America
91 90 89 88　　5 4 3 2

Library of Congress Cataloging-in-Publication Data

Hathaway, Dale E.
　Agriculture and the GATT.

　(Policy analyses in international economics ; 20)
　Bibliography: p 15
　1. Produce trade—Government policy—United States.　2. United States—Foreign economic relations.　3. Produce trade—Government
policy.　4. Tariff on farm produce.　5. General Agreement on Tariffs and Trade
(Organization).　6. Agriculture and state—United States.　I. Title.　II. Series.
HD9006.H28　1987　　382'.41'0973　　87–21430
ISBN 0–88132–052–8

Contents

Preface

Trade policy is a focal point of international economic attention in 1987 and for the foreseeable future, with new legislation under consideration in the United States Congress and the launching of the Uruguay Round of multilateral negotiations in the GATT. In an effort to contribute significantly to the debate, the Institute is simultaneously releasing studies on four major trade policy issues: agriculture, auction quotas (and the broader issue of implementing quantitative import controls), the politics of antiprotection, and textiles.

Agriculture is one of the most critical, and most complex, of all the trade policy issues now faced by the United States and its trading partners. It was addressed briefly in two earlier Institute studies: *Trading for Growth: The Next Round of Trade Negotiations*, by Gary Clyde Hufbauer and Jeffrey J. Schott, and in a chapter in *Trade Policy in the 1980s* by Dale E. Hathaway, the author of the current study. The need to resolve the problems of agricultural trade has been emphasized at the last two summit meetings, in Tokyo in May 1986 and in Venice in June 1987, and in the far-reaching proposals announced by the Reagan administration in July 1987. This analysis attempts to suggest a practical course of action through which agricultural trade policy can be successfully reformed in the Uruguay Round.

The Institute for International Economics is a private nonprofit research institution for the study and discussion of international economic policy. Its purpose is to analyze important issues in that area, and to develop and communicate practical new approaches for dealing with them. The Institute is completely nonpartisan.

The Institute was created by a generous commitment of funds from the German Marshall Fund of the United States in 1981, and continues to receive substantial support from that source. This study was partially funded by the Rockefeller Foundation, Rockefeller Brothers Fund, the World Bank, and Cargill, Incorporated.

In addition, major institutional grants are now being received from the

Ford Foundation, the William and Flora Hewlett Foundation, and the Alfred P. Sloan Foundation. The Dayton Hudson Foundation provides partial support for the Institute's program of studies on trade policy. A number of other foundations and private corporations are contributing to the increasing diversification of the Institute's financial resources.

The Board of Directors bears overall responsibility for the Institute and gives general guidance and approval to its research program—including identification of topics that are likely to become important to policymakers over the medium run (generally, one to three years) and which thus should be addressed by the Institute. The Director, working closely with the staff and outside Advisory Committee, is responsible for the development of particular projects and makes the final decision to publish an individual study.

The Institute hopes that its studies and other activities will contribute to building a stronger foundation for international economic policy around the world. Comments as to how it can best do so are invited from readers of these publications.

C. FRED BERGSTEN
Director
July 1987

1 Why Bother with Agricultural Trade Negotiations?

Differences in natural conditions and economic structures lead to great differences in cost of production of agricultural commodities from country to country. Normally such differences would lead to international trade that would allow world consumers to reap the gains possible from obtaining supplies from the low-cost producers. In agriculture, however, a complex web of intervention has developed for decades in many countries that make such gains impossible.

From their inception, the international trade rules relating to agriculture have been adjusted to fit the different national programs designed to protect farmers. Agriculture has been treated differently from other industries in the rules developed by the member nations of the General Agreement on Tariffs and Trade (GATT), and many of the trade practices common in agriculture have never had any effective rules applied to them.

This approach worked reasonably well for many years. But unusual events of the 1970s led to major changes in world trade flows in agriculture and in national agricultural programs. When world market conditions changed abruptly in the 1980s, the agricultural trade practices of a number of countries became increasingly important and disruptive to other countries and led to major confrontations and recriminations that have threatened to erupt into full-scale trade wars. At the same time, many of these domestic agricultural programs have been brought under scrutiny because of rising budget costs.

For years informed observers have believed that the trading rules in agriculture could not be made consistent and workable without fundamental adjustments in national agricultural programs. However, because of the powerful political influence of agricultural groups in major trading nations, these fundamental reforms have never been addressed directly in a GATT negotiation.

Now that situation has changed, and a new type of agricultural trade negotiation has been launched under the auspices of GATT. In September 1986 the Uruguay Round of multilateral trade negotiations (MTNs) was

1

officially launched—but only after major negotiations over the wording of the agricultural portion of the ministerial declaration. For the first time the member countries of the GATT agreed to negotiate on all agricultural programs that affect trade in agricultural products or limit access to markets. Despite a record of consistent disappointments regarding agricultural negotiations in past multilateral trade negotiations, a number of countries had made agricultural negotiations on fundamental reforms one of their top priorities in the new MTN. Even though the negotiations were officially launched in late 1986, a year later GATT members could not agree on the agenda or timetable for agricultural negotiations.

Given this long record of intractability, why is it important that the new round of GATT negotiations attempts fundamental reform in agriculture? There are three major reasons; each is important in its own right, but combined they make an overwhelming case for the high priority accorded agricultural trade negotiations. These are:

● National agricultural policies (which have a significant impact on agricultural trade) are under pressure in almost every country. Major changes will be easier politically if done multilaterally.

● Agricultural trade, still an important though declining share of world trade, has operated too long with inadequate GATT rules, thus undermining the very credibility of the GATT as an institution.

● Agricultural trade issues are an increasing source of friction between major trading partners. This tension could spread to other products and lead to a major trade war. Indeed, in each of the last several years there have been threats of a trade war between major trading nations over agricultural trade; only a series of last-minute settlements averted this clash.

Changes in National Policies

Agricultural policies are rooted in national history, often predating World War II and the GATT. Some policies grew out of the Great Depression and the food shortages right after World War II. Most of them were developed without regard to international trade or the GATT, at a time when domestic agricultural industries and economies were much different from what they are now.

For a variety of internal and external reasons, national agricultural policies are now under intense review. Experience in the 1970s and 1980s shows that many of these policies are expensive, disrupt trade, and fail to solve the problems they were designed to deal with. Because a significant number of these policies seem destined to change under major political and economic pressures at home, it is important that these changes have some consistency in terms of their future impact on agricultural trade.

At no time since World War II have so many countries been considering changes in their agricultural policies. It is in the interest of all countries that these changes take place with as little disruption as possible to their agricultural economies. Dislocations can be reduced if all major participants agree on direction and rules, and the GATT is the only effective negotiating forum to include the various countries concerned. Thus, even though these discussions will take the GATT in new directions, it is the right time and right place to shape appropriate national agricultural policies for the twenty-first century.

The Credibility of GATT

Even though the importance of agricultural products in world trade has declined relative to other goods, agricultural trade is still important, even crucial, for many countries. Despite the great gains in economic development in the last three decades, agriculture remains the major source of employment in many developing countries. In many cases, agricultural exports are the primary source of export earnings. For these countries, their own and the world's use of agricultural resources is a vital concern, as are the rules under which trade in agricultural products takes place.

Friction over agricultural trade has been growing partly because different rules exist for some countries and partly because the agreed rules are not being observed. Some GATT rules have also defied consistent interpretation. The result has been that the agricultural trading countries have come to view the GATT as irrelevant at best and a threat to their well-being at worst. Continual bickering over GATT rules for agriculture has eroded the credibility of the entire GATT dispute-settlement process. Unless credibility can be restored, this erosion of confidence will spread to other areas until no meaningful trade rules remain.

The success of agricultural negotiations also may be a crucial determinant of the success or failure of this round of trade negotiations. For many countries, this will be the issue upon which the outcome of the negotiations and its political acceptability will depend. Unless there is progress in agriculture, such countries will refuse to negotiate on other issues. Even in the United States, which has several key interests in the negotiations—including services, intellectual property rights, and investment—a failure of the agricultural negotiations would likely destroy the political base of support for the entire GATT round.

Trade Wars and International Cooperation

The experience of the 1980s has shown the extent to which agricultural trade tensions can erupt into wider arenas and other areas of international cooperation. This is not new. Many still remember the famous "chicken war" between the United States and the European Community (EC) in the 1960s, which threatened all trade and political cooperation among NATO allies. During the 1980s, Japan-US relations have been increasingly strained over agricultural trade issues. In the 1980s we have seen a steady escalation in policy actions designed to offset the actions of others that are asserted to be "unfair." Countries too small and too weak economically to engage in trade wars have seen their export earnings plummet and their economies crumble from the side effects of two years of guerrilla trade warfare between the United States and the EC in international grain markets. Unless some kind of permanent settlement can be reached, prospects are that these actions will increase.

However unimportant agricultural trade issues appear to many persons, especially in industrial economies, such chronic difficulties on these issues erode cooperation on other international problems. Australia has questioned its continued commitment to US defense installations because of US agricultural subsidies. US credibility on Caribbean Basin development has been undermined by the US sugar import policy. Just as war is too important to be left to generals, agricultural policy—especially as it affects trade—has become too important to be left to ministers of agriculture. The importance of completing a successful trade round that disarms trade disputes in agriculture extends beyond agriculture.

The Outline of the Study

This study attempts to lay out in nontechnical terms the agricultural issues in the new GATT round. An overview will be provided of the major policies followed by several dominant trading countries and the rationale behind these policies. This study covers the major GATT rules relating to agriculture, their history, and the difficulties experienced with them. The study concentrates on trade in major agricultural commodities, but this is not meant to imply that trade distortions occur only in these commodities. Quite the contrary is true. Some of the greatest transgressions occur in relatively insignificant products in the world economic order. But production of these commodities neither employs a significant portion of the world's agricultural resources nor makes up the bulk of agricultural trade.

There are several things that the study does not do. It does not contain any original estimates on the costs of the various agricultural trade distortions or the economic gains to be achieved from trade reform. Of the large number of studies available, most have been consulted and the general thrust of their results has been taken into account.

National agricultural policies and trade policies are usually examined separately. This study attempts to relate the two and to show how the interaction between them has led to a breakdown in the trading system in agriculture. It is hoped that it will improve understanding of issues that have been obscured and misstated for a long time.

2 From Food Crisis to Trade Crisis: Agricultural Trade, 1970–86

The agricultural trade crisis of the 1980s is rooted in economic and political developments of the 1970s and earlier. These developments include major shifts in agricultural trade patterns, incorrect projections of world supply and demand, and domestic farm policies and trade policies in numerous countries that evolved as a result of these changes.

World Trade in Agriculture

World trade in agricultural products is as old as commerce. Spices were one of the earliest goods sought from foreign lands. Tobacco was one of the first recorded exports from the new colonies in North America to England. The advent of large sailing ships brought the international movement of storable bulk commodities, such as wheat, wool, and tea.

Trade in agricultural products languished in the 1930s, as did trade in other products as the world experienced the Great Depression and the rise of protectionism. However, World War II and the massive disruption of shipping and overseas supplies put a new emphasis on self-sufficiency and expanding domestic production, especially in Great Britain, Western Europe, and Japan. In countries that had depended on outside food supplies, the old emphasis on overseas low-cost suppliers gave way to new domestic policies to encourage domestic farm output. Voters who had gone hungry in World War II said, "Never again."

Despite the rise of these self-sufficiency policies, trade in agricultural products expanded steadily, if slowly, in the 1950s and 1960s. The industrial countries grew rapidly, and rising incomes led to improved diets and expanding consumption of meat, poultry, and dairy products.

Starting in the 1960s, a new factor began to affect trade flows in agricultural products. Before and immediately after World War II, most agricultural trade was between developed countries, with a few developing countries exporting foodstuffs to developed countries. Cotton was a notable exception; it was

7

TABLE 2.1   **Volume of agricultural trade**
(metric tons)

Year	Total imports
1970	285,413,632
1975	357,386,496
1980	496,524,544
1981	518,666,752
1982	528,334,848
1983	531,221,504
1984	547,586,816
1985	542,151,168

Source: FAO Trade Yearbook 1961–86.

largely produced in developing countries and consumed in developed countries.

Rapid population growth and strong economic growth combined to increase demand for food faster than agricultural production in many developing countries in the 1960s, a trend that accelerated in the 1970s. In the early 1970s the Soviet Union became a major factor in the world market for grains when, in a basic policy change, it began to use imports to offset its internal production shortfalls. Other centrally planned economies followed a similar course.

This combination of world events, together with a modest decline in the world output of grains in the 1972/73 crop year, resulted in a sharp increase in volume traded and huge increases in the nominal and real prices of most traded agricultural products (tables 2.1 and 2.2). This combination of demand growth and export-supply response led to a marked change in world trade in agricultural products in the 1970s.

Export shares of developing countries fell sharply in 1960–80, while those of industrial market economies rose as sharply. The food trade balance of the industrial economies became positive and rose sharply while the balance of both developing countries and East European nonmarket economies turned increasingly negative through 1980.

This shift in trade patterns was most evident for grains but was not limited to them. In 1960/61 all developing countries (including China) imported a total of about 18 million metric tons of grain, Japan 5 million, the 10-nation European Community (EC-10) 21 million, other West European countries 4

T A B L E 2.2   **Food commodity prices and underlying factors, 1970–86**
(annual percentage change)

Year	Food commodity prices		Supply of food commodities[a]		
	Nominal (US dollars)	Real[b]	Production index	Supply index[c]	Closing stock index[d]
1970	5.1	−0.8	2.6	0.7	−23.3
1971	3.3	−1.5	7.1	2.7	4.6
1972	8.0	−0.4	−0.1	0.4	−17.4
1973	80.4	53.5	9.5	6.4	14.1
1974	23.6	3.1	−3.5	−1.9	−0.9
1975	−19.8	−29.4	6.3	5.6	16.4
1976	−6.2	−6.6	4.5	5.3	14.0
1977	−2.8	−10.5	2.7	4.0	3.3
1978	13.3	−1.7	7.7	6.9	12.9
1979	16.6	2.6	2.9	4.0	1.0
1980	8.6	−1.7	−1.0	−0.9	1.8
1981	−3.2	0.9	4.3	4.0	9.8
1982	−15.2	−13.4	5.0	5.5	17.1
1983	8.7	12.0	−3.8	−0.9	−16.1
1984	−0.7	2.1	7.9	4.7	23.0
1985	−15.5	−15.9	1.9	4.3	23.8
1986	−12.1	−25.6	3.3	5.7	11.3

Source: Commodities Division and Current Studies Division, IMF Research Department.
a. Group indices constructed using same weights for indices of individual food commodities as in group price index.
b. Deflated by unit values of manufactured exports.
c. Production plus beginning of year stocks.
d. End of (crop) year stocks.

million, and Eastern Europe 5 million.[1] The Soviet Union was a net exporter of 6 million tons! At that time, Western Europe was the major importer of wheat and coarse grains (table 2.3).

By 1972/73, a shift in patterns of world trade was already apparent and the events of the next two years brought it to world attention. By that time,

1. Agricultural production and trade statistics are generally reported on a crop-year basis using crops harvested in the Northern Hemisphere as the beginning year.

TABLE 2.3   **Net imports of wheat and coarse grains**[a]
(million metric tons)

Year	China	Japan	USSR	EC-10
1960/61	2.61	4.66	−6.24	21.06
1961/62	5.96	5.13	−8.15	23.71
1962/63	5.12	5.53	−8.03	19.87
1963/64	5.79	8.41	5.18	20.33
1964/65	4.96	8.57	−1.53	17.31
1965/66	6.11	8.58	3.69	21.62
1966/67	4.94	11.35	−1.96	20.26
1967/68	4.23	11.65	−4.42	18.56
1968/69	3.50	12.62	−6.18	15.76
1969/70	5.12	14.41	−6.27	13.55
1970/71	3.63	15.28	−7.53	22.18
1971/72	3.00	15.20	1.10	14.47
1972/73	5.97	17.49	20.87	12.85
1973/74	7.45	19.43	5.11	14.56
1974/75	5.91	18.49	0.23	12.25
1975/76	1.85	19.42	25.15	11.69
1976/77	2.93	21.38	7.30	21.82
1977/78	8.53	22.67	16.36	11.54
1978/79	11.05	23.53	12.54	6.50
1979/80	10.80	24.38	30.03	2.65
1980/81	14.44	24.57	33.50	−3.82
1981/82	14.32	23.74	45.80	−5.47
1982/83	15.60	24.24	32.80	−9.97
1983/84	9.48	26.06	31.60	−11.09
1984/85	1.54	26.05	54.48	−19.59
1985/86	0.06	26.82	28.90	−17.13

Source: Economic Research Service, USDA.
a. Trade years are July/June through 1975/76. Subsequently, trade year for course grain is October/September. Figures for 1985/86 are preliminary.
b. Includes India, Nepal, Bangladesh, Burma, Mali, Chad, Burkina Faso, Zaire, Burundi, Rwanda, Ethiopia, Uganda, Tanzania, Malawi, Haiti, Pakistan, Sri Lanka, Guinea, Ghana, Sierra Leone, Niger, Togo, Benin, Somalia, Kenya.

Other Western Europe	Eastern Europe	Low income[b]	Lower middle income[c]	Upper middle income[d]
3.97	5.08	6.12	5.68	6.38
3.36	5.95	4.73	6.96	7.28
4.57	7.85	5.81	6.82	6.45
4.40	8.10	6.45	6.16	6.48
3.97	7.83	8.79	5.89	4.38
6.48	6.65	10.41	5.46	4.25
6.28	3.32	13.19	8.04	7.16
4.14	3.37	10.70	8.06	6.64
3.55	2.90	5.65	7.91	7.18
4.18	3.32	5.60	8.05	7.07
5.18	9.84	5.14	8.62	8.98
4.47	7.90	5.22	11.57	13.10
4.89	5.72	5.65	14.91	15.83
7.63	5.61	8.46	17.02	18.19
6.93	7.09	10.41	18.60	19.86
6.54	8.74	11.49	18.12	18.94
7.58	10.55	7.99	20.04	20.76
9.11	9.49	4.22	27.12	29.34
8.78	12.90	5.35	26.65	30.21
10.47	13.30	4.74	35.07	37.49
8.00	13.72	4.07	34.27	36.34
13.24	9.28	5.90	28.70	30.62
8.94	2.84	6.21	36.03	37.93
7.53	2.38	7.71	39.51	42.17
4.31	−0.15	7.77	38.36	41.01
0.44	3.47	5.48	30.58	33.44

c. Includes El Salvador, Honduras, Bolivia, Thailand, Indonesia, Philippines, Egypt, Sudan, Mauritania, Senegal, Nigeria, Zambia, Zimbabwe, Lesotho, Guatemala, Nicaragua, Costa Rica, Jamaica, Dominican Republic, Colombia, Ecuador, Peru, Turkey, Morocco, Tunisia, Cameroon, Ivory Coast, Congo Republic.
d. Includes Mexico, Panama, Trinidad, Venezuela, Chile, Brazil, Uruguay, Portugal, Greece, Syria, Iraq, Iran, Israel, Jordan, Malaysia, Singapore, South Korea, Hong Kong, Algeria.

developing countries, including China, were importing about 34 million tons, Japan 17.5 million tons, the EC-10 only 13 million tons, and the Soviet Union, suddenly, 21 million tons. In a relatively short period, developing countries, Japan, and the Soviet Union became the major importers. The volume of world grain trade jumped a quarter from 1971/72 to 1972/73. Prices of traded wheat, corn, and rice doubled in nominal dollar terms. By 1974 the price of rice was more than three times its 1972 level, the prices of wheat and corn over two and one-half times their 1972 level. The International Monetary Fund (IMF) index of food commodity prices rose 80 percent in nominal dollar terms and 54 percent in real terms.

The combination of these trade shifts, the sharp rises in real prices of food commodities, and a decline in world food output, together with the first "oil shock," led to near panic among policymakers, economists, and many others concerned with world food trade. The first reaction of most national policymakers was to attempt to isolate their domestic economies from the world market changes. The United States imposed a short-supply embargo on soybeans, the EC imposed export levies to prevent outflows of grains, Japan signed a supply-purchase agreement with the United States (the Butz–Abe Agreement), and after a partial supply embargo by the United States in 1975, so did the Soviet Union.

The Club of Rome predicted continuing food shortages and rising real prices. Worldwatch predicted widespread starvation in developing countries; prominent meteorologists said the climate had changed permanently in ways that reduced crop output, and the United Nations called an emergency World Food Conference in late 1974. There were widespread calls for persons in affluent economies to reduce red meat consumption to make grain available for consumption by poor people in developing countries.

In retrospect, the situation never was quite the way it was generally depicted, and the predictions of world calamity never came true. World grain consumption went up in 1973, not down, as stocks were drawn from then record levels. World production rebounded in response to higher prices and a removal of US production restraints. It was not until adverse weather in 1974 cut grain output in the United States and the USSR that world grain consumption actually declined, but it still remained well above any previous year but one (1973). The IMF index of food commodity supply, which combines production and stocks (table 2.2), shows that world food supply fell only once from the previous year's level in the 1970s.

Real prices of food commodities were a better indicator of what was happening than were either press reports or most economic analyses. Nominal prices for cereals peaked in 1974 and fell markedly over the next two years before rising again. Prices of food commodities in real dollars *fell* in 8 years during the 1970s, but nominal price increases in 7 of the 10 years gave a different impression.

Policy responses and private investment decisions did not respond as quickly as markets, but they did respond. The general policy response was to take actions that would encourage agricultural output in both importing and exporting countries. Policy actions included raising price guarantees to farmers, expanding irrigation and drainage areas, providing low-cost fertilizer, subsidizing public credit, and building new import or export facilities. Where public policies encouraged it, or did not prevent it, private investment was used to expand planted areas, to build new plants to turn out machinery and fertilizer, and to promote the rapid adoption of practices to increase yields. In the early 1960s about 650 million hectares of grain were harvested per year worldwide. By 1975 this had increased to approximately 700 million hectares, and harvested area in grains peaked at 734 million hectares in 1981/82.

World trade in grains peaked in 1980/81 at 215 million tons, almost exactly three times the volume of 1960/61. But the trade at that time was quite different from what it had been two decades earlier. Developing countries, including China, were importing 73 million tons, the USSR 39 million tons, and Eastern Europe 12 million tons. The EC was a *net exporter* of 4 million tons by this time.

Thus, in a period of 20 years, the trade patterns for agricultural products had been transformed. The USSR and Eastern Europe shifted from net exporters to net importers of over 40 million tons of grain annually. Japan increased its imports by about 20 million tons annually. Developing countries went from being modest importers to the largest group of importers. Over this period, the importance of trade increased significantly as trade in grains rose from 8.6 percent of world consumption in 1960/61 to 11.2 percent in 1973/74, and to 14.7 percent in 1980/81. Confident predictions were made that trade would account for 20 percent of consumption by 1985—predictions that proved wrong. In fact, by 1985/86 world trade in grains fell to 12.3 percent of consumption.

Macroeconomic Changes Bring New Trade Patterns

Agricultural trade in the 1970s and 1980s also has been subjected to a number of macroeconomic changes that have further destabilized an industry already buffeted by major changes in supply, demand, and trade. Perhaps most important of these was the move from fixed to floating exchange rates in the early 1970s and the subsequent large movements in the relative value of currencies of many agricultural trading countries.

Most agricultural trade in the major bulk commodities is priced in dollars because of the dominant position of both US agricultural exports and the dollar. Agricultural producers and exporters in most countries, however, operate in their local currencies; therefore, the price received by local producers reflects not only the current world price in dollars but also the exchange rate between their local currency and dollars.

For an indication of the immense effects of exchange rate changes, see table 2.4, which shows the IMF commodity price index in dollars, special drawing rights (SDRs), and selected currencies. While commodity prices in US dollars fell rather steadily from 1980 to 1985; in pounds sterling they rose 65 percent to the first quarter of 1985; in deutsche marks, 42 percent; and in French francs, 86 percent.

This means that while the world price for US wheat producers (who produce and sell in US dollars) was declining sharply, for German, British, and French wheat producers the world price was rising. What is not shown in this case is that since the Australian and Canadian dollars also were falling markedly against the US dollar, wheat prices were rising over most of the period for their producers also.

These currency changes profoundly affected the actual levels of protection offered by various agricultural policies. At the peak of the exchange rate between the dollar and the European currency unit (ECU) in 1984/85, the internal prices of agricultural products under the EC's common agricultural policy (CAP) were only moderately above world dollar prices, and the export subsidies per unit of product fell without a reduction in internal prices. Conversely, between early 1985 and early 1987 the internal prices under the CAP rose sharply relative to world prices without any appreciable increase in internal prices—and even though some internal prices had declined.

Other macroeconomic factors that have a major impact upon agricultural production and trade are inflation and real interest rates. During a period such as the 1970s, when price inflation generally was high and real interest rates were low or negative, both helped to fuel the boom in world agriculture. Because modern agricultural production is very capital intensive, low or negative real interest rates lower production costs and make it easier to expand output. Moreover, in a period of high inflation and low or negative real interest rates, the accumulation and holding of commodity stocks is

TABLE 2.4 **Commodity prices in selected currencies, 1960–86**[a]

	Indices (1980 = 100)						Rate SDR-US dollar exchange rate
Year	US dollar	Pound sterling	Deutsche mark	French franc	Japanese yen	SDR	
1960–69	33.2	28.6	73.4	39.0	52.8	43.3	1.000
1970–79	63.4	69.9	87.6	70.7	76.9	70.2	0.871
1980–86	84.7	121.2	112.4	136.8	84.5	98.3	0.896
1970	37.1	35.9	74.7	48.8	58.9	48.3	1.000
1971	36.1	34.5	69.4	47.4	55.7	46.9	0.997
1972	38.8	36.1	68.1	46.4	51.9	46.5	0.921
1973	63.1	59.8	92.8	66.6	75.6	68.9	0.839
1974	76.3	75.8	108.6	86.9	98.3	82.6	0.831
1975	63.9	67.1	86.5	64.8	83.7	68.5	0.824
1976	69.3	89.7	96.1	78.4	90.7	78.2	0.866
1977	76.7	102.2	98.0	89.2	90.9	85.5	0.857
1978	77.8	94.3	86.0	83.1	72.2	80.9	0.799
1979	94.5	103.7	95.3	95.2	91.3	95.2	0.774
1980	100.0	100.0	100.0	100.0	100.0	100.0	0.768
1981	89.9	104.0	111.8	115.6	87.5	99.3	0.848
1982	80.6	107.2	107.6	125.3	88.5	95.0	0.906
1983	85.6	131.2	120.2	154.4	89.7	104.2	0.935
1984	87.4	152.7	136.6	180.8	91.6	111.0	0.976
1985	76.0	138.0	123.4	161.6	80.0	97.4	0.985
1986[b]	73.1	115.9	87.6	119.8	54.3	81.1	0.852
1984:Q1	91.0	147.4	135.3	178.8	92.6	112.9	0.953
Q2	92.7	154.3	138.3	182.8	93.9	115.4	0.956
Q3	84.8	151.8	136.1	179.7	91.0	109.0	0.988
Q4	81.3	155.3	136.5	180.1	88.1	106.4	1.006
1985:Q1	79.1	165.0	141.7	186.4	89.8	106.4	1.034
Q2	77.6	143.5	131.8	172.8	85.8	101.8	1.008
Q3	72.9	123.3	114.3	150.0	76.7	92.4	0.974
Q4	74.4	120.3	105.8	138.9	67.9	89.8	0.927
1986:Q1	77.7	125.4	100.3	132.5	64.3	89.9	0.889
Q2	74.5	114.7	92.0	126.0	55.9	83.5	0.861
Q3	69.8	108.8	80.1	111.9	47.9	75.5	0.831
Q4	70.5	114.6	77.8	109.6	49.8	76.1	0.829
1987:Q1	70.5	108.6	72.9	104.4	48.6	74.3	0.793

Source: IMF, Commodities Division of the Research Department, *Primary Commodities: Market Developments and Outlook*. Washington, May 1987.
a. Commodity prices are measured by the IMF price index that comprises 39 price series for 34 nonfuel primary commodities. See appendix 1 of IMF, *Primary Commodities: Market Developments and Outlook*, 1986, for a description of this index. Data relate to a "world" index, that is, to a single basket of primary commodities and do not reflect differences in the composition of the basket of primary commodities imported by different countries.
b. Includes projections for the final quarter of the year.

costless or relatively inexpensive. Conversely, falling nominal commodity prices and high real interest rates make the holding of commodity stocks prohibitively expensive for the private sector.

In addition to the output and inventory effects of inflation and low real interest rates, these factors plus rising expectations fueled a worldwide boom in agricultural land prices. The subsequent collapse of these prices in the 1980s in a number of countries, including the United States, turned the commodity price decline into a financial crisis in many agricultural areas.

Markedly different resource endowments, agricultural structures, climate, and history have always made agricultural policy coordination difficult. The addition of new macroeconomic elements has now made it substantially more complex, if not impossible.

The economic situation in the 1980s turned out to be quite different from the one in the 1970s and quite different from expectations when policies were formed and investments made in agricultural production and related industries. World economic growth slowed, world trade growth slowed, but world agricultural production continued to grow in response to high prices and productive investment.

In 1982 world trade in most agricultural products began to fall after nearly two decades of steady increases. But an increasing number of countries had by this time enacted policies designed to encourage output expansion, much of it intended to meet a rising export demand that was not there.

As export markets stagnated and production increased, the competition for these markets increased, and the food crisis turned into a trade crisis. As production increasingly exceeded domestic market demand, EC exports expanded in the 1980s with the help of export subsidies. Canada, Australia, and Argentina expanded their export volumes in the early 1980s. At the same time, the export volume of the United States, which had become the world's largest agricultural exporter, fell drastically. US market share and export earnings fell even more drastically.

As exports fell, the price support mechanisms in many countries became operative and a massive stock accumulation began to occur in major agricultural commodities. In many cases the problem of stock accumulation was dealt with by exporting the excess supply, usually with the aid of large export subsidies.

By the mid-1980s India, Pakistan, Saudi Arabia, and Great Britain, which had been major importers in the 1970s, all became wheat exporters. China became a corn exporter. Pakistan, Taiwan, China, and Indonesia became rice exporters. In 1985 the United States reentered the direct export subsidy competition in a major way. Changes in US domestic legislation put even more pressure on world markets as the country sought to regain market share by drastically lowering prices and using export subsidies. (These major policy changes are covered in the next chapter.)

The growth in world agricultural output was interrupted by a massive land retirement program in the United States and a drought there in 1983 that reduced yields on the fewer acres. The US output reduction was enough to cause the sharpest recorded decline in the IMF index of food production since 1970. But unlike in 1973, the resultant price rises were modest and short lived. In 1984/85 an increase in Soviet grain imports to 55 million tons brought a one-year blip in world grain trade, which then fell to the lowest level since 1979. The nominal price of cereals in US dollars, which had risen in 7 of the 10 years of the inflationary period of the 1970s, began to fall in the 1980s. The fall accelerated in 1985 and 1986 as US support prices were lowered.

The increased use of export subsidies and falling commodity prices have brought rising international tension. The leaders of Argentina, Australia, Canada, Thailand, and several other countries have publicly protested the expansion of government subsidies in world agricultural trade and finally organized a group to push their concerns in the GATT negotiations. As markets shrank, exporters' protests against the import barriers of a number of countries rose. Attempts to settle some of the more difficult disputes over sugar, wheat flour, wheat, and pasta in the General Agreement on Tariffs and Trade (GATT) have not satisfied many of the parties concerned. Thus, there are widespread calls for reform of the GATT rules for agriculture.

It is important to understand that the trade crisis is real in both political and economic terms. It has caused a plunge in agricultural export earnings for countries as varied as Argentina, Australia, Canada, the United States, and Thailand. In a number of countries where government subsidies do not protect farm income, the income of farm producers has fallen sharply. In those countries that have programs to protect farm income, the program costs have skyrocketed and their sustainability is questioned.

The history of agricultural production and trade over the last 25 years has been one of overreaction, overproduction and domestic policies that attempt to avoid adjustment to changing world market conditions. In the 1960s there was modest overcapacity in agriculture, largely in the United States as a result of its expansion during and immediately after World War II. However, in much of the world there was underinvestment in agriculture at that time. In the 1970s a unique set of events led to the belief that the capacity of world agriculture and associated industries needed to be expanded greatly and rapidly. Domestic agricultural policies around the world were changed to induce greater output. In many countries policies in the 1980s are still geared to encouraging output expansion, even though additional output is not needed. As world trade growth has slowed, overcapacity has erupted into trade disputes as each country has attempted to avoid adjusting its agricultural system to the changed market situation.

This situation was recognized in an official statement signed by the leaders of the major industrial nations at the Tokyo economic summit on 6 May 1986. It said:

We note with concern that a situation of global structural surplus now exists for some important agricultural products, arising partly from technological improvements, partly from changes in the world market situation, and partly from long-standing policies of domestic subsidy and protection of agriculture in all our countries. This harms the economies of certain developing countries and is likely to aggravate the risk of wider protectionist pressures. This is a problem which we all share and can be dealt with only in cooperation with each other. We all recognize the importance of agriculture to the well-being of rural communities, but we are agreed that, when there are surpluses, action is needed to redirect policies and adjust structure of agricultural production in the light of world demand. We recognize the importance of understanding these issues and express our determination to give full support to the work of the OECD [Organization for Economic Cooperation and Development] in this field.

It is important to understand that:

● National agricultural policies developed in the 1970s in order to expand output are no longer appropriate, given the present and prospective world market situations.

● National policies now operating are transferring the excess capacity into major trade problems.

● Major changes in trade policy without attendant changes in domestic policies will not deal with the problem.

● Even fundamental changes in long-run policies will not deal with the current short-run problem of substantial excess capacity relative to world demand.

These distinctions are important because there is a widespread belief that changes in trade rules alone will reverse the recent downward trend in the world prices of agricultural commodities. The combination of excess capacity and predatory trade policies clearly has destabilized world commodity markets and forced prices below their equilibrium levels. This does not mean, however, that the long-term prospects are for stable or rising real prices of agricultural commodities. The fact is that the long-term trend in real agricultural commodity prices is down and, until or unless there is a marked decline in the development and use of new productivity-increasing technology, prospects are that this trend will continue. Historically, there have been substantial price variations in agricultural commodities, with periodic rises and falls in real agricultural prices that diverged for a few years at a time from the basic long-term downward trend. These variations are likely to occur again because of the nature of agricultural markets; and they are likely to be pronounced at times if national policies continue to work against economic forces by trying to prevent domestic price increases when shortages occur and domestic price declines in periods of surplus. These policies accentuate the price fluctuations in world trade and exacerbate the problems of producers and consumers in open economies, even though they may stabilize farm prices and incomes in the protected economies.

3 Production and Trade in Commodities

Ideally, the agricultural trade rules that are agreed upon in the present round of trade negotiations should apply uniformly across all commodities. However, these are political negotiations, not economic negotiations. Because of their relative economic and political importance to key countries and because of the friction they cause in agricultural trade, some commodities will receive special attention in the agricultural negotiations. Other commodities will be given undue attention because of their great importance to influential political constituencies, despite their relative insignificance in trade. Some commodities will escape attention for the same reason.

Consequently, the negotiations will focus on certain products. Unless accommodation can be reached on these products, the negotiations will fail. It is, therefore, useful to outline recent trends of major agricultural commodities in international trade, some of the issues arising with these commodities, and the national interests involved.

Grains

Grains are the key to agricultural trade negotiations for several reasons. In terms of agricultural production, the arable land area devoted to grains far exceeds that devoted to production of any other agricultural crop. Nearly 600 million hectares of grains are harvested annually, with some production in nearly every country in the world.

Grains are also an essential foodstuff in many countries. In low-income developing countries direct human consumption of grains is still the largest single source of calories. Rice in particular is still the staple food in many Asian developing countries. Wheat is a staple food in several countries as well, and in some areas coarse grains are consumed directly as food. Coarse grains and wheat also are a primary source of feed for livestock, dairy animals, and poultry under most modern production conditions.

21

As a result, grains, especially wheat and coarse grains, are widely traded. In 1984/85 over 200 million tons of wheat and coarse grains were traded, a sixth of all the grain then consumed. This trade is both a major source of export earnings for many countries and a major source of conflict in agricultural trade.

Wheat and coarse grains should be considered together since they are competitive in both production and use in many countries. While wheat is often considered to be food for humans, in many areas of the world it is produced primarily for animal feed. Conversely, while most coarse grains are considered to be animal feedstuffs, in some parts of the world they are an important source of human food.

The aggregate trends in world wheat and coarse grain production, consumption, and trade are shown in table 3.1.* World production and consumption have both increased over the years, with much of the production increase due to higher yields per hectare. World trade expanded rapidly in the 1970s while world stock levels were drawn down drastically. The situation changed in the 1980s. As production continued to expand, consumption expanded less rapidly, resulting in an increase of stocks to the highest levels ever—both in absolute levels and relative to consumption.

A more precise picture can be obtained by examining separately production and trade patterns of wheat and coarse grains. Even though they are related, each has a different pattern of trade.

WHEAT

World production of wheat is widespread, although a few countries dominate production. Since 1970 both China and the European Community (EC) have expanded wheat production substantially. In good years China and the USSR are the largest producers followed by the EC, the United States, India, Canada, and Australia. These seven producers account for approximately 75 percent of world production (table 3.2).

The world price of wheat has reflected supply, demand, and trade conditions in the commodity (figure 3.1). The nominal price of wheat was relatively stable in the 1950s and 1960s, rose sharply in the 1970s, and has declined rather steadily in the 1980s. The real price, however, declined steadily and markedly through the 1950s and 1960s, more than doubled from 1971 to 1974, and has declined more or less steadily since 1974. By 1986 the real price of wheat was only one-third the level of 1974.

---

*ED. NOTE: *All tables in this chapter are presented as a group, beginning on page 43.*

FIGURE 3.1   **Wheat prices** (dollars per metric ton)

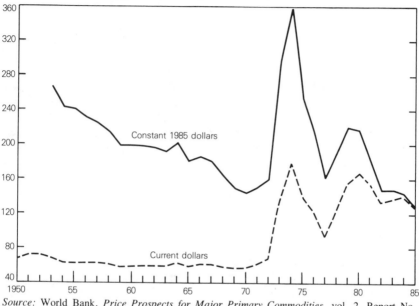

Source: World Bank, *Price Prospects for Major Primary Commodities*, vol. 2, Report No. 814186, October 1986.

The isolation of world wheat production from these price changes can be seen by the fact that among the top five world wheat producers only the United States has allowed internal market prices to follow world prices. But even in the United States, wheat producers have been protected from price declines by target-price payments. It is worth noting that among the largest producers only the United States has reduced production in the 1980s.

The export trade for wheat is even more concentrated than is production, and only two of the top exporters are among the largest producers—the United States and France (table 3.3). The major exporters are the United States, Canada, the EC (France), Australia, and Argentina. These five account for over 80 percent of all exports. During the 1980s the two leaders, the United States and Canada, have seen a decline in their exports, while exports from France, Australia, and Argentina have continued to rise.

Market share of world exports has become a focal point of trade disputes in the 1980s for, as we shall see, the current General Agreement on Tariffs and Trade (GATT) rules make it an important issue when subsidies are involved. Market shares of wheat trade for the top five exporters are shown in table 3.4. The US market share rose rapidly in the 1970s and has fallen as rapidly in the 1980s to even below 1970 levels. The market shares of Argentina, Australia, and the EC have risen significantly over the last decade.

Imports of wheat are dispersed among a number of countries, although those of the Soviet Union have come to dominate the market, accounting for as much as a quarter of world trade in peak years (table 3.3). The largest single importer in 1970—the United Kingdom—has now become a net exporter. India, the second largest importer in 1975, has also become a net exporter. Four of the top five importers in 1985 use state trading for wheat imports, while the fifth is in the EC. Thus, internal markets in all are insulated from world price changes.

COARSE GRAINS

World coarse grain production (over 800 million tons annually) is nearly twice as large as world wheat production. The United States leads with nearly one-third of world production. Other major producers have consistently been the USSR, the EC, China, Eastern Europe, India, Canada, and Argentina. These eight producers account for approximately 80 percent of world coarse grain production in a normal year (table 3.5). The top five coarse grain producers—the United States, USSR, China, India, and France—have all increased output in the 1980s.

Trade in coarse grain is concentrated on the exporter side as well (table 3.6). As with wheat, the United States has consistently been the leading exporter, followed by Argentina, the EC (France), China, Canada, and Australia. The export position for coarse grains remained more or less stable until 1984. The same five countries (which were the top five exporters in 1970) retained their positions over most of that period. The United States alone accounted for nearly 60 percent of world exports in the late 1970s, but has since dropped to as low as 38 percent in 1985/86. In addition, China displaced Canada and Australia in 1984 and 1985. Australia, China, and France have all increased both absolute levels and market shares of exports in the 1980s (table 3.7).

Perhaps the most striking change in coarse grain trade can be seen in the import market. In 1970 the top five importers were Japan and four current Common Market countries—Germany, Italy, the United Kingdom, and the Netherlands. Imports of coarse grains by the EC countries have fallen steadily

FIGURE 3.2 **Corn prices** (dollars per metric ton)

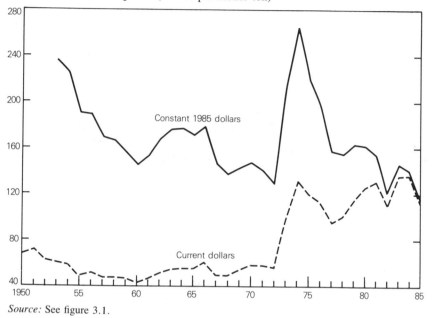

Source: See figure 3.1.

as domestic production displaced imports. World imports became widely dispersed as the EC moved from a net importer to a net exporter and the USSR suddenly increased its imports. By 1985 the top five importers were Japan, the USSR, Saudia Arabia, Taiwan, and South Korea.

Price changes in world coarse grain markets have been similar to wheat but somewhat less volatile (figure 3.2, figure 3.3). It is generally agreed that the price elasticity of demand is higher for coarse grains than for wheat. Also, a lower proportion of world trade in coarse grains is subject to state trading or quantitative import restrictions. Even so, the nominal price of coarse grains is well below the highs of the 1970s, and the real price is less than half of a decade earlier.

Table 3.8 shows the shift in export market shares of wheat and coarse grains combined. The US market share dropped sharply during the 1980s to a low of 32 percent in 1985/86. The EC market share increased from 17 percent in the late 1970s to between 21 percent and 25 percent in the mid-1980s. The market share held by Australia, Argentina, and Canada combined

FIGURE 3.3   **Sorghum prices** (dollars per metric ton)

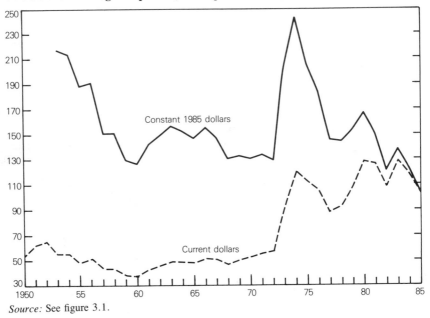

Source: See figure 3.1.

went up from about 25 percent in the late 1970s to over 30 percent in the mid-1980s. Other exporters, namely China, Thailand, and South Africa, increased their combined share from between 7 percent and 11 percent in the 1970s to between 14 percent and 16 percent in the 1980s. In other words, several countries picked up market shares in this period of declining trade in the 1980s, and many of them did so without benefit of export subsidies.

The importance of grains in agricultural production and consumption has made them a prime candidate for governmental intervention in most countries. Wheat and corn were designated "basic commodities" in US agricultural legislation more than fifty years ago, and both observers of and participants in the EC common agricultural policy (CAP) have remarked upon the favored position of grain producers in the EC. These policies have become very expensive to both the United States and the EC in recent years.

These subsidies have, in turn, become the chief bone of contention in agricultural trade discussions. Critics have argued that the EC shift from a net importer of 25 million tons of grain in 1976/77 to a net exporter of 15 million tons or more a decade later is the result of the high internal prices given to domestic producers without regard to the world market. With these high internal prices, no EC grain could be exported in the absence of an export subsidy, and competing exporters have complained loudly and bitterly about increasing EC competition in world markets during a period of declining trade.

These trends in trade of wheat and feed grains indicate why policies for grains are important to both the EC and to other exporters. France has long been a major producer of grain as well as an exporter. Initially, its exports primarily moved to fill the import needs of its European neighbors. But now, protected by the CAP, several other EC countries are rapidly approaching self-sufficiency in grains, so that the only remaining markets for French grain are external to the EC with the aid of export subsidies. Outside exporters find they have not only lost the EC market, but also face rising competition in other world markets from subsidized EC grains.

The wheat and coarse grains are clearly important to the trade negotiations. Grains policy is the keystone of agricultural policy in the United States, the EC, Canada, Australia, and Argentina. The price of grains is a key factor in livestock, dairy, and poultry production costs and thus becomes critical to trade in those commodities. Grains are a vital component of the export earnings of Australia, Argentina, Canada, France, and the United States. Thus, these countries will seek some settlement of grain issues as a minimum achievement in the negotiations.

Major importing countries also have an important interest in the outcome of any changes in grains policy. Some of them, such as Japan, Korea, and the USSR, have been major beneficiaries of the low world market prices created by the excess grains supplies and subsidy wars. Many other importers, especially among developing countries, have found it easy in recent years to continue to underprice grains in their domestic markets. By making use of subsidized imports, they retard the income and growth of their domestic agricultural sectors.

RICE

Production and trade patterns in rice are markedly different than for other grains. The world's major rice producers are China, India, Indonesia, Bangladesh, Thailand, and Japan (table 3.9). But only two of these countries,

Thailand and China, are long-term major rice exporters (China has become the fourth largest exporter in the last decade).

With two notable exceptions, rice exporters are developing countries. The exceptions are the United States, which produces only 4 million to 5 million tons annually, less than 2 percent of total world production, and Italy, which produces less than one-half of 1 percent of world production. Despite their modest production levels, the United States has consistently been the world's second largest exporter behind Thailand, and Italy now is the fifth leading exporter (table 3.10).

Thailand, which has produced and exported without benefit of extensive subsidies, has nearly doubled its market share in rice trade in the past two decades (table 3.11). China, currently the fourth largest exporter, has steadily gained market share in the 1980s. The United States has lost market share in the 1980s, both in absolute and relative terms.

On the import side, only one of the top five importers of rice in 1970—Vietnam—was still in the top five in 1985 (table 3.10). Four of the top five importers in 1985—Brazil, Iran, Iraq, and Saudia Arabia—were only modest importers in 1970. Unlike many importers of wheat and coarse grains, most rice-importing countries are not heavily dependent upon imports.

Rice prices in the world have shown a different trend and greater volatility than either wheat or coarse grains. The nominal price of rice did not decline significantly in the 1950s and 1960s, and the real price declined even less (figure 3.4). Both the nominal and the real price shot up in the 1970s. However, in the 1980s both have declined markedly. The real price of rice in 1986 was less than one-fifth of the 1974 peak and down by over one-half from 1981, and only about one-third the level of the 1960s.

Production and trade in rice have not followed the path of wheat and coarse grains. Even though world rice production and consumption have expanded, most of the expansion in consumption has not been through trade. Even at its peak, world rice trade never exceeded 3 percent of world production, compared with 22 percent for wheat and 15 percent for coarse grains. Thus, the international rice market is thin and highly volatile. Widespread government intervention in both domestic and international rice markets adds to this volatility.

Much of the controversy over rice policy centers upon Japan, which neither imports nor exports rice. Japan is still a major producer and consumer of rice, although per capita consumption has been declining slowly for nearly two decades. Japan's self-sufficiency in rice is obtained at a very high cost

FIGURE 3.4 **Rice prices** (dollars per metric ton)

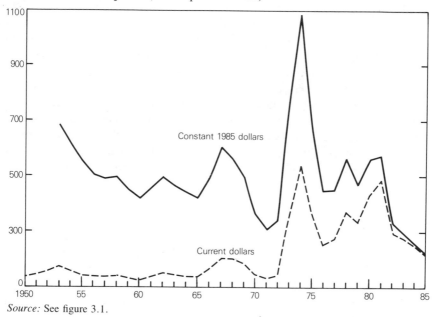

Source: See figure 3.1.

in terms of both producer and consumer prices. Japanese producer prices—the world's highest—are 8 to 10 times world prices. Consumer prices are only slightly lower because of an expensive subsidy.

US rice producers have asserted that if Japan opened its rice market and brought internal prices down to world levels, domestic production would fall, consumption would rise, and imports would rise sharply. Given the high production costs for rice in Japan, a reduction in domestic prices probably would result in significantly lower production and a substantial dependence upon imports. But it is doubtful that lower prices would stimulate consumption markedly in this high-income, well-fed country where the price elasticity for rice is low and the income elasticity is probably negative.

The Japanese have strongly resisted reducing protection for their rice producers because of the vital position of rice production in Japanese farm income and because of the Japanese desire for self-sufficiency in this basic food grain. Rice policy in Japan is probably the strongest case of food security driven price policy that can be found in the world today. These concerns were amplified by the shortages and export embargoes of the 1970s that reminded Japan of its vulnerability.

Another major controversy involves the massive US subsidy program for the production and export of rice, which is strongly resented and bitterly opposed by other exporters, most of which are developing countries.

Both US and Japanese policies work to put downward pressures on world prices by subsidizing production that would not otherwise occur, and by stimulating exports (the United States) and limiting imports (Japan). In the area of rice policy, the two major opponents are likely to be the United States and Japan, although the big gainers in a negotiation that resulted in subsidy reductions by these two countries would be other producers and exporters.

GRAIN SUBSTITUTES

A group of products known as grain substitutes has become important in world trade. These products are tapioca, corn gluten feed, and citrus pellets. Their importance has grown in part because of protection for other products. They now have become a major point of contention in agricultural trade and must be dealt with in the context of grains.

Tapioca is a starchy root produced and consumed by the lowest-income rural people in tropical developing countries. It contains carbohydrates and is very low in protein. In recent years it has been developed as an animal feed and has become a major feed ingredient (using soybean meal as the source of protein) imported by the EC. Thailand has become the major producer and exporter of tapioca for feed. Corn gluten feed is the by-product of the wet-corn milling industry, which produces high fructose sweetener, ethanol, and other products from corn. It contains both carbohydrates and protein. Citrus pellets, a by-product of the citrus juice industry, consist of the dried pulp remaining after juice extraction and also contain carbohydrates and proteins.

These products have two things in common. Along with oilseeds, they are of substantial value in livestock feed rations. These grain substitutes also have tariffs bound at zero or near zero levels by the European Community under the Dillon Round of tariff negotiations.

In the EC, high internal prices and variable levies on grain have resulted in a massive import of these products for use in mixed feeds. As grain surpluses have developed in the EC (requiring expensive intervention and export subsidy programs), EC grain producers have urged restrictions on the importation of grain substitutes. EC producers and policymakers correctly argue that these levy-free imports substitute for grain in feed rations, thereby adding to the EC grain surpluses. Outside suppliers of these substitutes and EC feed users correctly observe that the costs are the result of high internal grain prices.

The EC has repeatedly suggested ways of "completing the CAP," that is, placing tariffs or levies on these substitutes. As the major exporter of corn gluten feed, the United States has vigorously opposed such restrictions as a violation of trade agreements paid for in earlier rounds of trade negotiations.

In 1984 the EC imposed a "voluntary" restraint agreement on Thailand under which the Thais agreed to cut exports of tapioca to the EC from 8.5 million to 5.5 million tons per year. The Thais were resentful, but claim they had no alternative but to accept the agreement in lieu of more drastic action by a powerful trade partner. The United States has, thus far, resisted similar restraints on other grain substitutes, even when offered some promise of compensation.

The issue is not settled. In early 1987 Canada determined that US subsidies on corn constituted a countervailable subsidy of 85 cents per bushel. It was later reported that French corn growers would file a similar case in an attempt to impose a duty on corn gluten feed, charging that it was subsidized by the US programs for corn and sugar. If a countervailing duty were to be placed upon corn gluten, it would almost certainly precipitate a major crisis between the United States and the EC that would bring the issue to GATT and fully into the trade negotiations.

Both political and economic considerations will require that grain substitutes be dealt with along with grains. The major participants will be the EC, as the only major importer, and the United States, Thailand, and Brazil as interested exporters. The solution to these issues, however, will have a significant impact upon EC grain export policies, which, of course, are of interest to a larger group of exporters.

Oilseeds

Oilseeds and their products are another major group of agricultural commodities that are important in world trade. The major oilseeds are palm, coconut, soybeans, rapeseed, sunflower, and cottonseed. Apart from some modest direct human consumption of soybeans in China and Japan, the oilseeds are produced for their two components: vegetable oil and protein meal. Vegetable oils are widely consumed by humans as cooking oil and margarine, and in a variety of food and nonfood items. The protein meals are used largely as a protein source in animal and poultry feeds, in combination with grains, tapioca, and other products low in protein.

The production of oilseeds is widely spread among countries (table 3.12). Palm oil production is dominated by Malaysia, with some production in a number of other tropical developing countries. Soybean production is heavily concentrated in the United States, Brazil, and Argentina. Rapeseed is produced largely in Western Europe and Eastern Europe, including the USSR. Sunflower is produced in Western Europe, the USSR, and Argentina.

The United States is the largest oilseed producer, followed by China, Brazil, India, Argentina, and the USSR. Outside the centrally planned economies, world oilseed production, with a few notable exceptions, has been affected relatively less by direct government subsidies than has been the case for grains. For instance, in Japan and Korea, which have very high levels of border protection for many agricultural products, soybeans and products enter at world prices. One notable exception has been the EC, which initiated an oilseed policy in the late 1970s specifically intended to encourage the domestic production of oilseeds to displace imports. Since the duties on seeds and products are bound at very low levels, the policy is achieved by payments to oilseed processors to compensate them for paying EC producer prices that are well above world prices.

Export trade in seeds is dominated by the United States, with Argentina, Canada, China, Brazil, and increasingly France as important exporters. The EC, in particular France, and Argentina have increased exports markedly since 1970. Importers of seeds are the EC, Japan, the USSR, Taiwan, Mexico, and South Korea. World trade in seeds peaked in the early 1980s, after growing rapidly in the 1970s, and has been below peak levels for four consecutive years (table 3.13).

Production and trade flows in oilseed products are complicated by the fact that, while all oilseed production is shown in a single statistic, it consists of seeds with widely varying oil and meal content, and much of the trade occurs in the form of products. This is due partially to the fact that a number of producing countries use differential export taxes to encourage processing of the seeds within the country. Also, both vegetable oils and meals have a relatively high income elasticity, and therefore both consumption and production have grown rapidly over the past fifteen years.

The production of oilmeals is widely dispersed, although the United States dominates production. The EC, Brazil, China, the USSR, India, Argentina, and Japan are other significant producers. Meal production has continued to climb, paralleling the output of seeds (table 3.12).

Trade in meal is dominated by EC imports, which account for nearly two-thirds of all meal imports (table 3.14). Eastern Europe is the only other area with large oilmeal imports. Exports of meal are led by Brazil, the United States, Argentina, the EC, China, Chile, and India (table 3.14). EC exports have been growing faster than imports, so that the net import position of the EC is declining.

Production of vegetable oils has a different pattern from meals because of the importance of palm oil. Approximately 40 percent of all vegetable oil production occurs in Asia, with Malaysia the leader. Oil production is also large in the United States, the EC, the USSR, Brazil, and Argentina.

Trade in oil varies markedly from trade in seeds or meals. India is now the world's largest importer of vegetable oils after the EC. The United States, Pakistan, and Singapore have all increased their imports as well. Malaysian exports have increased markedly since 1972 and now dominate all vegetable oil exports. The EC, Argentina, the Philippines, and the United States are other significant exporters (table 3.15). US exports have fallen in the 1980s, whereas those of EC countries, Malaysia, and Argentina have risen sharply. World prices of vegetable oils have fallen sharply as supply increases have exceeded demand growth (figure 3.15).

The impact of the EC oilseed subsidy program can be seen in production and trade flows. EC oilseed production has risen sharply in response to high producer prices. Imports of seeds for crushing have declined as domestic production has risen. The EC oilseeds program is structured to ensure that domestic seeds are processed and used in the EC. Imports of meal for feed use have leveled off as domestic meal production has risen, and EC processors have become an increasing force in export markets. This leaves the outside suppliers to compete in the remaining world markets.

The barriers to oilseed trade are less than for many other products, but they still will be important issues in the negotiations. Seeds such as soybeans, sunflower, and rape are grown on land that also can produce grains. The EC wants to increase oilseed production to divert land from grains. However, in the absence of import levies, the oilseed program is very costly per unit of land used. That cost could be reduced markedly if an import levy on oilseeds and products could be used to increase internal prices.

The most recent proposal was a stiff tax on all vegetable oils in the EC,

FIGURE 3.5 **Soybean oil prices** (dollars per metric ton)

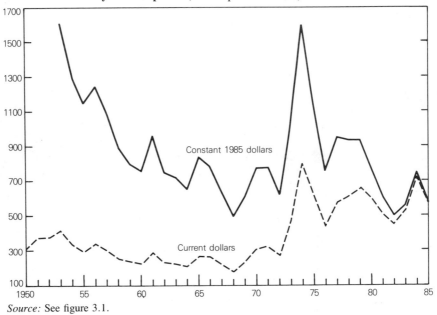

Source: See figure 3.1.

including olive oil, with the proceeds to be used to pay for the costly domestic oilseed program. The tax would have two desirable effects from the point of view of EC policymakers. It would skew prices in favor of animal fats, especially butter, and help reduce dairy surpluses. And it would provide large revenues to finance expansion of local oilseed production to displace imports of seeds, meal, and oil, and reduce the costs of grain surpluses.

Not surprisingly, the proposed tax was strongly attacked by other exporters of seeds, oils, and meals. The United States threatened to retaliate if the tax were adopted. This highly controversial proposal was finally laid aside by the EC heads of state in June 1987.

In addition to the EC subsidies, US subsidies on oil exports, and some other trade-distorting practices, there are differential import taxes on processed products in importing countries and differential export taxes in many exporting countries. These are all efforts to protect local processing industries. They have been a major trade irritant in the recent past and will continue to be so in a period of excess processing capacity.

Dairy Products

Dairy products are unique in a number of ways, not least the high degree of protection accorded them by almost every country. They are consumed in a variety of forms including fluid milk, butter, cheese, and nonfat dry milk. Since fluid milk cannot easily be stored for long periods, is expensive to transport, and is consumed directly by humans, much of the production occurs close to where it is consumed. Almost all trade in dairy products takes place in the form of manufactured products—butter, cheese, and nonfat dry milk.

Most of world milk production is in the EC, the USSR, and the United States (table 3.16). Only a few developing countries have significant milk production, namely India, Brazil, and Mexico. However, wherever they are located, dairy producers receive one of the highest levels of protection of any major group of agricultural producers.

Since fluid milk is not storable and is not traded, the imbalances between dairy production and consumption show up in production and trade in manufactured dairy products. Butter, cheese, and nonfat dry milk, in addition to the fluid milk, are manufactured to meet market demand for these products. When excess supplies of fluid milk appear, they are usually directed to the manufacture of products. Where dairy price support programs exist, they normally take the form of supporting the price of the manufactured products.

The production of manufactured dairy products parallels milk production, with some important differences. Butter production is largely concentrated in Europe, including the USSR (table 3.16). However, India, which produces only 5 percent of world milk output, makes 11 percent of world butter, while the United States, with 15 percent of world milk output, makes only 7 percent of world butter.

World butter consumption has grown slowly over the past two decades because of the availability of low-cost vegetable oils as a source of dietary fats and oils. As a result, butter is one of the few products where trade in the mid-1980s is actually lower than in 1970 and where a high proportion of the trade involves government subsidies. The biggest shifts in world butter markets have been:

• the change in the EC from the world's largest importer to the world's largest exporter

• the rise of the United States as an exporter

• the emergence of the Soviet Union as the dominant importer (table 3.17).

The loss of traditional markets in Western Europe to domestic producers, and the rise of subsidized exports, have been a difficult blow to New Zealand, which has not had significant subsidies for its dairy industry but is almost totally dependent upon exports. The main beneficiaries of these expensive domestic and export subsidy programs have been dairy producers in Europe and the United States, and the consumers in the Soviet Union.

World cheese production and consumption have grown quite rapidly in the 1970s and 1980s (table 3.16). As with other dairy products, cheese production is heavily concentrated in Europe, the USSR, and the United States. World cheese trade has dropped sharply because of the EC's shift from a net importer to a net exporter (using the EC as a single unit). The United States and Japan have increased imports in both absolute and relative terms (table 3.18).

World nonfat dry milk production and consumption have risen slowly also over the past decade (table 3.16). The EC (in particular France and West Germany), the United States, the USSR, New Zealand, and Japan are the largest producers. Here, as in butter, world trade also has declined, and the EC has shifted from a large importer to a large exporter via subsidies. The United States has also expanded its exports via subsidies, while New Zealand has struggled to maintain its market position (table 3.19). The decline in imports of nonfat milk by developed countries has been partially offset by the emergence of Mexico, India, South America, and the USSR as importers.

Apart from sugar, the protection of dairy producers is more pervasive than for any other agricultural product. However, dairy product exports are of major importance to only a few producers, especially New Zealand, Australia, and the EC. Exports provide an outlet for surplus disposal to the EC and the United States. Developing-country interest in the trade, either as exporters or importers, probably is quite low. Thus, to a large extent, dairy trade is likely to be an issue confined to a relatively few developed countries.

Dairy production adjustment has an important side effect beyond dairy products. Dairy animals are the largest users of animal feeds in the United States and Western Europe and are a major source of beef and veal. Thus, what happens in dairy programs is of great importance to grain, oilseed, and beef producers.

Beef and Veal

There is an important relationship between beef and veal production and dairy production in much of the world. This is because a substantial proportion of the beef output comes either from dairy cows or from dairy calves raised for meat.

World beef and veal production rose sharply in the early 1970s and remained relatively constant in the early 1980s. The same five countries— the United States, the USSR, Argentina, Brazil, and France—have been the top producers over the past two decades (table 3.20).

The top five exporters are not all the major producers, nor are they the same as in 1970 and 1975. Australia and New Zealand have long been significant exporters, but traditional exporters like Argentina, Uruguay, and Ireland have been displaced by Brazil, France, and Germany (table 3.21). Argentina, which in 1970 had one-fourth of the export market, has been pushed out, as it lost its traditional markets in EC countries to domestic producers. The Community became a net exporter of beef in 1980 and recently displaced Australia as the largest exporter (table 3.22).

The United States and the USSR, though the two largest producers, also are among the largest importers (table 3.21). US imports have been relatively flat, while those of the USSR and Japan have grown rapidly. Total world trade has increased only moderately in the past twenty years. Beef and veal trade is complicated by animal health issues that do not affect most other products. The United States and Japan import only fresh and frozen products from countries certified free of hoof and mouth disease. This excludes most Latin American and European countries.

Beef trade is another area in which great disparities in producer protection exist. A number of the major exporters, namely Argentina, Australia, New Zealand, Uruguay, and Brazil, have no producer subsidies. Japan, Korea, and Taiwan have very high producer protection through import quotas, and the United States has used quotas or voluntary restraint agreements intermittently to control imports. The EC programs have provided both import protection and export subsidies to producers. Thus, the lines in these issues will be between countries with significant producer subsidies and those without. As in the case of grains, beef trade is also of great importance to a number of developing countries because of their apparent comparative advantage in beef production.

Pork

Since 1970 world pork production has doubled, in large part due to the enormous growth of Chinese production (table 3.23). Pork is another commodity in which the largest producers are not always the major trading nations. Of the top producers—China, the United States, the USSR, West Germany, and France—only China is among the major exporters, which also include Denmark, the Netherlands, Belgium, the German Democratic Republic, Canada, and Hungary (table 3.24). The EC became a net exporter of pork in the late 1970s and has moved to become the world's largest exporter in a short period.

Unlike with beef, some EC countries traditionally were major exporters of pork prior to their entry into the Common Market. Their position in this regard has not changed significantly and thus their market share of world trade has not increased (table 3.25). What has happened, however, is that production in other EC countries has grown to fill domestic demand, so that more of the traditional exporters' production has been directed to markets outside the EC.

The major importers of pork have traditionally been West Germany, the United Kingdom, Italy, France, and the United States. However, imports in Japan, the USSR, and Hong Kong have risen significantly in recent years, so that together these importers make up 20 percent of the market.

Trade in pork differs from beef trade in another way as well. Apart from China, pork trade does not involve developing countries in a significant way, either as importers or exporters. However, pork production is a major user of grains; and, thus, any changes that occur will have a significant effect upon grain use.

Poultry

The production of poultry meat is the most rapidly expanding portion of meat production. In the 1970s, poultry production nearly doubled and has continued to increase in the 1980s as the worldwide decline in real prices has stimulated consumption (table 3.26). The five largest producers in 1985—the United States, the EC (France), the USSR, Brazil, Japan—have all expanded output; but the expansion has been especially rapid in Brazil and Japan.

Poultry trade patterns also have changed markedly over the past decade and a half (table 3.27). As is the case in other products, the EC went from a net importer to the largest net exporter, primarily because the French share in world trade increased fourfold. Brazil went from zero to the second largest exporter in the last decade. The US share of world exports rose sharply in the late 1970s and then fell as sharply in the 1980s in response to the rise in EC and Brazilian exports (table 3.28).

On the import side, only West Germany has maintained its position as the world's largest importer, although its imports now come from within the EC instead of outside it. Saudi Arabia, the USSR, Hong Kong, and Japan, respectively in that order, have become the other leading importers, with Hong Kong depending largely on nearby Chinese suppliers.

After rapidly increasing in the 1970s, world poultry trade has leveled off. Since 1983 it has remained relatively stable as production technology has proven to be easily transferred to countries where demand is growing. Major exporters therefore must compete vigorously for a static market, and new entrants such as Thailand and Taiwan threaten traditional exporters.

The trade negotiations will be primarily between competing exporters who subsidize and those who do not. Since poultry production costs are heavily dependent upon feed cost, the need for subsidies or protection or both is closely related to protection for feed grains. Even though modern poultry meat production is relatively capital intensive, processing still requires a substantial labor input and, thus, developing countries with high technology and low wages have an increasing advantage.

Sugar

Production and trade in sugar are unique in several ways. World sugar production is widely dispersed, although much of it occurs only because of the high levels of protection given to producers in developed countries. Sugar is also unique in that it faces severe competition from other sweetener products and because it has been developed as a major source of nonfood products, such as ethanol, in some countries.

World sugar production and consumption grew rapidly in the 1970s with immense swings in prices over the decade. Production continued to climb in the 1980s, even though world consumption growth slowed (table 3.29). As a result, stocks grew, prices plummeted in world markets, and trade declined. In 1985 the real price of sugar was 7 percent of its 1974 peak, and only 11 percent of the 1980 price and well below any price in the post–World War II period (figure 3.6).

Sugar comes from sugar cane and sugar beets. Cane is produced in tropical or subtropical climates in Asia, South America, the Caribbean, Africa, and North America. Sugar beets are produced largely in Western and Eastern Europe, the USSR, and North America.

FIGURE 3.6   **Sugar prices** (dollars per metric ton)

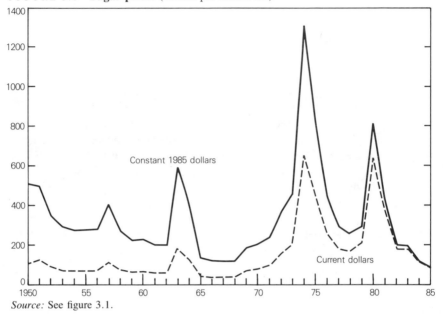

Source: See figure 3.1.

Traditionally, sugar trade occurred between the low-cost tropical producing areas and the developed consuming areas of Western Europe, North America, and Japan. This trade pattern has been changed drastically by agricultural policies in the traditional importing countries and by technology, which developed sugar substitutes under the umbrella of these agricultural policies (table 3.30).

At the beginning of the 1970s the United States was the single largest sugar importer under a system that fixed internal prices, domestic production, and imports. That system was changed in 1974 to one that supported internal prices, had no domestic production controls, and left imports to fill the market residual. At the same time, high fructose corn syrup (HFCS) was developed and, under the protection of the high domestic sweetener price, moved quickly to replace sugar in the domestic sweetener market. As a result, sugar consumption per capita in the United States has declined by 30 percent since 1979, and sugar's share of the domestic sweetener market declined from 72 percent to 43 percent from 1978 to 1985. Sugar imports by the United States dropped by half from 1980 to 1985, and could go to zero by 1990. By 1985, all sweeteners in soft drinks in the United States came from nonsugar sources.

The second major policy-induced blow to world sugar trade was the CAP of the EC. In 1967 the 12 countries now making up the EC were net importers of nearly 4 million tons of sugar. Between 1967 and the 1980s, however, domestic sugar production doubled under the protection of the CAP, and by the mid-1980s the EC was the world's largest exporter of sugar (with total exports of over 6 million tons and net exports of 4.5 million tons). The EC makes much of two facts—that it continues to import more than 2 million tons of sugar from former colonies and that part of its export subsidies is paid by domestic producers. It has ignored the total impact of its program on world production and trade patterns, and has refused to accept GATT findings against its programs.

Japan's sugar program is similar to many of its other programs. Domestic producers receive prices several times the world price, and import controls reduce low-cost imports. Despite rising consumption levels, imports have fallen.

The EC and Japan, among others, have controlled the use of substitute sweeteners, especially high fructose corn syrup produced from corn. If, however, protection and controls over sugar production and trade were removed, it now appears that the producers of HFCS would be competitive in many sweetener markets, especially the large US market where investment in production facilities has already been made and low raw material costs result in low marginal cost of protection.

The losers in the sugar situation have been the developing countries that are low-cost cane producers and Australia. These include Brazil, India, the Philippines, Thailand, and a number of very poor African and Caribbean countries. Every study shows that removing sugar protection programs in the United States, the EC, and Japan would produce greater gains for developing countries than any other change in levels of agricultural protection. Other important gains from such changes would involve consumers in Western Europe, the United States, and Japan.

Despite all of these arguments for change, the prospects are not bright. Protection for domestic sugar producers is deeply rooted in the agricultural policy histories of the United States, the EC, and Japan. Moreover, sugar is a commodity where none of these big three will gain substantially from changes in policies of the others. Thus, domestic producer pressures in all three countries will be to avoid change, and none will have producer pressures to push for change.

Cotton

Cotton is the most important nonfood agricultural commodity produced and traded (lumber and rubber are forest products). Unlike other agricultural commodities, cotton experienced no world boom in production and trade during the 1970s. Indeed, apart from year-to-year fluctuations, both production and trade were flat over the decade.

Cotton is unique in another respect also. Probably because it cannot be produced in most developed countries, cotton production has less protection and fewer direct subsidies than almost any other major agricultural commodity. The notable exception is in the United States, where farm programs have affected cotton since the 1930s. Until the 1980s, when the US government programs became an important factor, subsidies as such were not an important issue in cotton trade.

The world's major producers of cotton are China, the United States, the USSR, India, and Pakistan (table 3.31). Cotton production and exports also are important in a number of other developing countries. The leading exporters of cotton have been the United States and the USSR. Recently Pakistan, China, and Australia have increased their exports; together they held approximately 15 percent of the market in 1985, while in 1970 they held less than 4 percent.

The major importers of cotton are the EC, Japan, South Korea, Taiwan, and Hong Kong (table 3.32). Since none of the major importers are producers, cotton is one of the few products where protection of domestic producers in importing countries is not a significant issue in world trade. Thus, cotton is one of the few agricultural products where the United States has t'ie major subsidy program.

Trade and Trade Negotiations

An overall view of commodity trade indicates quite clearly the interests and countries likely to play a key role in the agricultural negotiations. The grains-oilseeds-livestock complex is the key to the negotiations for several reasons. Together these commodities account for the bulk of the trade important to both exporters and importers. This complex also encompasses crucial interests of both developing- and developed-country exporters.

Because of their important position in both production and trade in these commodities, it is clear that the interests of the United States, the EC, Canada, and Australia must be met. Many of the developing countries share similar interests with those of some of the larger exporters.

For certain commodities, such as sugar, rice, and cotton, the production and trade patterns are quite different. Progress on these commodities will depend upon either the application of uniform changes arising from the other products or upon the ability of developing country coalitions to persuade some of the developed-country producers to change policies.

There also is a group of tropical products such as coffee, tea, and tropical fruit which are important export earners for developing countries. For these products the issues are different. They do not face competition from subsidized production in temperate zone countries, but they do face problems of differential tariffs and access barriers that limit access of processed products. Negotiations on these items will be largely a one-on-one negotiation with a heavy North-South flavor.

TABLE 3.1 **World supply and demand of wheat and coarse grains**
(million metric tons)

Year	Area harvested (hectares)	Yield	Production	World trade[c]	Utilization total[d]	Ending stocks[e]
1960/61	526.6	1.30	686.3	65.9	672.0	191.5
1961/62	525.8	1.25	659.0	76.8	685.6	164.9
1962/63	527.8	1.35	711.4	75.4	709.6	166.6
1963/64	531.2	1.32	701.7	90.0	702.6	165.7
1964/65	537.7	1.38	743.5	87.0	742.0	167.2
1965/66	535.6	1.40	748.0	103.0	782.1	130.4
1966/67	534.7	1.55	827.2	96.0	799.3	158.3
1967/68	545.7	1.55	848.4	89.9	830.8	175.9
1968/69	549.8	1.61	883.5	82.0	854.4	205.0
1969/70	548.2	1.62	885.6	89.1	902.6	188.0
1970/71	538.3	1.65	888.8	101.0	929.4	147.5
1971/72	545.4	1.80	980.1	101.3	959.7	167.9
1972/73	536.8	1.77	951.3	126.2	986.6	132.4
1973/74	561.2	1.86	1,044.4	134.0	1,040.3	135.9
1974/75	561.9	1.76	991.2	129.3	995.2	130.4
1975/76	574.7	1.74	1,002.6	141.9	1,000.5	130.3
1976/77	577.9	1.95	1,126.2	147.1	1,071.0	185.9
1977/78	573.6	1.89	1,085.7	161.6	1,091.5	179.6
1978/79	572.7	2.10	1,202.0	164.7	1,177.0	204.4
1979/80	571.9	2.04	1,169.0	185.2	1,187.2	186.1
1980/81	579.1	2.03	1,175.0	202.9	1,187.7	173.6

T A B L E 3.1   *(continued)*

Year	Area harvested (hectares)	Yield	Production	World trade [c]	Utilization total [d]	Ending stocks [e]
1981/82	588.8	2.06	1,215.8	197.9	1,181.9	207.5
1982/83	577.1	2.19	1,261.5	188.6	1,215.0	254.1
1983/84	564.0	2.09	1,176.1	195.1	1,243.8	186.5
1984/85	566.4	2.34	1,325.4	207.6	1,278.6	233.3
1985/86	569.6	2.36	1,344.5	168.3	1,257.9	319.7
1986/87[a]	567.0	2.41	1,368.3	178.0	1,317.8	370.2
1987/88[b]	497.5	2.65	1,319.1	186.9	1,328.4	360.9

Source: Foreign Agricultural Service, US Department of Agriculture, Washington.
a. 1986/87 data are preliminary.
b. 1987/88 data are projected.
c. Trade data as expressed in this table exclude intra-EC trade. Wheat and coarse grains are on a July/June trade year through 1975/76. From 1976/77 the trade year for coarse grains is October/September.
d. For countries for which stock data are not available (excluding the USSR), utilization estimates represent apparent utilization, i.e., include annual stock level adjustments.
e. Stocks data are based on an aggregate of differing local marketing years and should not be construed as representing world stock levels at a fixed point in time. Stocks data are not available for all countries and exclude those such as the People's Republic of China and parts of Eastern Europe. World stocks levels have been adjusted for estimated year-to-year changes in USSR grain stocks, but do not purport to include the absolute level of USSR grain stocks.

T A B L E 3.2   **Wheat production**
(million metric tons)

	1970/71	1975/76	1980/81	1981/82	1982/83	1983/84	1984/85	1985/86[a]
China	29.2	45.3	55.2	59.6	68.4	81.4	87.8	85.8
USSR	99.7	66.2	98.2	81.1	84.3	77.5	68.6	78.1
EC-12	41.3	45.1	61.5	58.1	64.7	63.8	82.9	71.7
France	12.9	15.0	23.7	22.9	25.4	24.8	33.2	29.3
United States	36.8	57.9	64.8	75.8	75.3	65.9	70.6	66.0
India	20.1	24.1	31.8	36.3	37.5	42.8	45.5	44.1
Canada	9.0	17.1	19.3	24.8	26.8	26.5	21.2	24.3
World	313.7	356.6	443.0	449.5	477.3	489.3	511.5	498.8

Source: See table 3.1.
a. Figures for 1985/86 are preliminary.

TABLE 3.3 **World wheat trade**[a]
(million metric tons)

	1970/71	1975/76	1980/81	1981/82	1982/83	1983/84	1984/85	1985/86
Exports								
United States	20.2	31.9	41.2	48.2	39.9	38.9	38.1	25.0
Canada	11.9	12.3	16.3	18.5	21.4	21.8	19.4	16.8
EC-12	3.4	8.4	15.7	15.7	16.3	15.5	18.5	15.6
EC-12[b]	5.8	14.5	21.7	22.3	21.9	22.3	28.4	27.8
France	3.2	8.8	13.4	13.3	13.1	14.0	18.8	17.0
Australia	9.1	8.7	9.6	11.0	8.1	10.6	15.8	16.0
Argentina	1.0	3.2	3.9	3.6	7.5	9.7	8.0	6.1
Imports								
USSR	0.5	10.1	16.0	20.3	20.8	20.5	28.1	15.7
China	3.7	2.2	13.8	13.2	13.0	9.6	7.4	6.6
Egypt	2.8	3.8	5.4	5.9	5.5	6.7	6.6	6.3
Japan	4.8	5.9	5.8	5.6	5.8	5.9	5.6	5.5
EC-12	9.5	5.4	5.6	5.6	4.6	4.0	3.4	2.9
EC-12[b]	12.7	12.3	11.4	12.1	10.1	10.9	13.0	15.0
Italy	1.5	2.1	3.0	3.5	2.4	3.2	4.5	5.3
World[b]	56.5	74.0	96.9	107.8	107.0	110.0	115.9	96.1
World[c]	55.0	66.7	94.1	101.3	98.7	102.0	107.0	84.9

Source: See table 3.1.
a. Wheat is on a July/June trade year. Figures for 1985/86 are preliminary.
b. Figures include intra-EC-12 trade.
c. Figures exclude intra-EC-12 trade.

TABLE 3.4   **Market share of exports for wheat**[a]
(percentage)

	1970/71	1975/76	1980/81	1981/82	1982/83	1983/84	1984/85	1985/86
United States	35.8	43.1	42.5	44.7	37.3	35.4	32.9	26.0
Canada	21.1	16.6	16.8	17.2	20.0	19.8	16.7	17.5
France	5.7	11.9	13.8	12.3	12.2	12.7	16.2	17.7
Australia	16.1	11.8	9.9	10.2	7.6	9.6	13.6	16.6
Argentina	1.8	4.3	4.0	3.3	7.0	8.8	6.9	6.3
EC-12	10.3	19.6	22.4	20.5	20.7	20.3	24.5	28.9

Source: See table 3.1.
a. Market shares calculated using figures that include intra-EC trade (see table 3.3).

TABLE 3.5   **Coarse grain production**
(million metric tons)

	1970/71	1975/76	1980/81	1981/82	1982/83	1983/84	1984/85	1985/86[a]
United States	146.1	185.5	198.3	246.6	250.7	137.1	237.7	274.9
USSR	76.9	65.8	80.5	69.4	91.8	101.9	90.5	100.0
EC-12	61.3	71.1	82.6	76.1	80.7	73.9	89.6	88.3
France	18.7	20.7	24.2	22.1	23.3	21.5	25.2	26.8
China	64.5	68.9	82.4	79.5	81.6	91.6	96.2	82.3
Eastern Europe	42.6	57.8	60.4	62.1	69.3	66.9	72.8	68.3
India	30.5	30.4	28.5	31.4	27.9	33.9	31.5	26.1
Canada	19.5	20.0	22.1	26.0	26.5	20.9	22.0	25.0
Argentina	15.6	12.4	21.0	18.4	17.8	17.1	18.9	17.1
World	575.2	646.1	732.9	766.0	784.4	686.8	814.0	845.7

Source: See table 3.1.
a. Figures for 1985/86 are preliminary.

TABLE 3.6 **World coarse grain trade**[a]
(million metric tons)

	1970/71	1975/76	1980/81	1981/82	1982/83	1983/84	1984/85	1985/86
Exports								
United States	18.6	49.3	70.7	60.0	54.0	55.7	55.4	36.4
Argentina	9.1	6.9	14.4	11.5	11.6	10.9	10.6	9.7
EC-12	3.3	4.4	5.9	4.0	4.2	4.3	8.5	8.1
EC-12[b]	8.6	12.6	15.0	14.4	15.0	14.7	19.0	19.7
France	5.7	6.5	7.4	6.7	7.6	8.3	9.8	9.9
China	0.03	0.4	0.2	0.2	0.1	0.3	6.0	7.1
Canada	4.3	5.0	4.8	7.5	7.1	5.5	3.3	5.8
Australia	2.9	3.7	2.4	3.0	0.9	5.4	6.4	5.0
Imports								
Japan	10.5	13.5	18.9	18.3	18.7	20.7	20.7	21.5
USSR	0.3	15.6	18.0	26.0	11.0	11.9	27.3	13.5
Saudi Arabia	0.03	0.2	2.7	4.2	3.5	5.9	5.5	7.4
EC-12	19.2	17.1	19.7	18.6	14.3	12.2	9.6	5.5
EC-12[b]	27.3	31.8	28.3	30.4	25.9	23.2	20.8	18.3
Taiwan	0.9	2.3	3.7	3.9	4.2	4.0	4.3	4.1
South Korea	0.3	0.9	2.4	3.2	4.2	4.2	3.4	4.0
World[b]	54.3	87.4	119.0	109.3	96.5	103.0	112.8	95.8
World[c]	46.0	75.2	107.8	96.6	89.9	93.1	100.7	83.3

Source: See table 3.1.
a. Coarse grain trade is on a July/June trade year through 1975/76. Subsequently the trade year is October/September. Figures for 1985/86 are preliminary.
b. Figures include intra-EC-12 trade.
c. Figures exclude intra-EC-12 trade.

TABLE 3.7   **Market share of exports for coarse grains**[a]
(percentage)

	1970/71	1975/76	1980/81	1981/82	1982/83	1983/84	1984/85	1985/86
United States	34.3	56.4	59.4	54.9	56.0	54.1	49.1	38.0
France	10.5	7.4	6.2	6.1	7.9	8.1	8.7	10.3
Argentina	16.8	7.9	12.1	10.5	12.0	10.6	9.4	10.1
China	0.1	0.4	0.2	0.2	0.1	0.3	5.3	7.4
Canada	7.9	5.7	4.0	6.9	7.4	5.3	2.9	6.1
Australia	5.3	1.2	2.0	2.8	1.0	5.2	5.7	5.3
EC-12	15.8	14.4	12.6	13.2	15.5	14.3	16.8	20.5

a. Market shares calculated using figures that include intra-EC trade (see table 3.6).

TABLE 3.8   **Market share of exports for wheat and coarse grains**[a]
(percentage)

	1970/71	1975/76	1980/81	1981/82	1982/83	1983/84	1984/85	1985/86
United States	35.0	50.3	51.8	49.8	46.2	44.4	40.8	32.0
France	8.0	9.5	9.6	9.2	10.2	10.5	12.5	14.0
Canada	14.6	10.7	9.8	12.0	14.0	12.8	9.9	11.8
Australia	10.8	7.7	5.6	6.4	4.4	7.4	9.6	11.0
Argentina	9.1	6.3	8.5	7.0	9.4	9.7	8.1	8.2
EC-12	13.0	16.8	17.0	16.9	18.1	17.4	20.7	24.9

a. All market shares calculated using figures that include intra-EC trade (see tables 3.3, 3.6).

TABLE 3.9   **Milled rice production**[a]
(million metric tons)

	1970/71	1975/76	1980/81	1981/82	1982/83	1983/84	1984/85	1985/86
China	77.0	87.9	97.9	100.8	112.9	118.2	124.8	117.9
India	42.2	48.7	53.6	53.3	47.1	60.1	58.3	64.2
Indonesia	13.1	15.2	20.2	22.3	22.8	24.0	25.9	26.5
Bangladesh	11.1	12.8	13.9	13.6	14.2	14.5	14.6	15.0
Thailand	9.0	10.1	11.5	11.7	11.1	12.9	13.1	13.0
Japan	11.6	12.0	8.9	9.3	9.4	9.4	10.8	10.6
World	213.3	243.6	271.2	281.2	286.2	308.7	319.2	320.1

Source: See table 3.1.
a. The world rice harvest stretches over six to eight months. Thus, 1980/81 production represents the crop harvested in late 1980 and early 1981 in the Northern Hemisphere and the crop harvested in early 1980 in the Southern Hemisphere. Figures for 1985/86 are preliminary.

TABLE 3.10   **World rice trade**[a]
(thousand metric tons)

	1971	1976	1981	1982	1983	1984	1985	1986
Exports								
Thailand	1,576	1,870	3,049	3,620	3,700	4,528	3,993	4,338
United States	1,461	1,732	3,028	2,682	2,331	2,129	1,906	2,389
Pakistan	182	763	1,163	840	1,299	1,050	962	1,146
China	1,292	897	590	470	580	1,168	1,010	950
Italy	260	423	475	544	485	436	631	667
Burma	844	657	674	701	750	727	450	636
Imports								
Brazil	1	0	0	180	326	0	400	1,250
Iran	60	276	583	587	680	730	600	450
Iraq	97	198	350	369	474	490	475	500
Saudi Arabia	202	189	356	427	491	530	500	500
Vietnam	600	805	30	150	30	300	400	500
World	8,446	10,166	13,233	12,185	11,924	12,558	11,475	12,712

Source: See table 3.1.
a. Trade data on calendar year basis. Figures for 1986 are preliminary.

TABLE 3.11   **Market share of rice exports**[a]
(percentage)

	1971	1976	1981	1982	1983	1984	1985	1986
Thailand	18.7	18.4	23.0	29.7	31.0	36.1	34.8	34.1
United States	17.3	17.0	22.9	22.0	19.5	17.0	16.6	18.8
Pakistan	2.2	7.5	8.8	6.9	10.9	8.4	8.4	9.0
China	15.3	8.6	4.5	3.9	4.9	9.3	8.8	7.5
Italy	3.1	4.2	3.6	4.5	4.1	3.5	5.5	5.2
Burma	10.0	6.5	5.1	5.8	6.3	5.8	3.9	5.0

a. Market shares calculated from table 3.10.

TABLE 3.12   **Major oilseed, oilmeal, vegetable and marine oil production**[a]
(million metric tons)

	1972/73	1975/76	1980/81	1981/82	1982/83	1983/84	1984/85	1985/86[b]
Oilseed production								
United States	41.7	47.8	55.9	64.0	68.2	50.4	59.2	65.4
China	13.5	15.3	19.5	23.6	26.1	27.3	31.1	31.6
Brazil	6.8	12.5	16.7	14.4	16.2	16.8	20.4	15.4
India	9.1	12.1	11.0	14.0	12.0	14.0	15.1	13.9
Argentina	2.2	2.8	5.8	7.3	7.8	10.5	11.3	12.4
USSR	9.8	10.9	10.4	10.6	11.2	10.8	10.0	10.8
EC-12	1.9	1.9	3.3	3.3	4.5	4.6	6.3	7.1
World	111.8	132.9	155.1	169.5	178.3	165.7	191.0	195.8
Oilmeal production								
United States	18.2	20.9	24.8	25.2	26.7	22.6	24.8	25.1
EC-12	8.6	11.2	14.1	15.6	15.5	14.0	14.3	15.0
Brazil	2.8	5.4	11.3	10.6	10.7	10.3	11.7	10.3
China	3.4	3.9	5.3	6.9	8.0	7.9	9.1	9.3
USSR	4.9	5.9	5.5	5.7	5.6	5.3	5.1	6.2
India	3.6	4.4	4.4	5.4	4.9	5.5	6.5	5.9
Argentina	1.1	1.2	1.9	2.9	3.6	4.4	4.7	5.5
Japan	3.5	3.4	4.4	4.5	4.7	4.9	5.0	5.0
World	58.0	70.2	88.8	94.6	97.6	93.4	102.0	103.8
Vegetable and marine oil production								
United States	4.7	5.3	6.2	6.2	6.6	5.8	6.3	6.4
EC-12	4.2	5.3	6.1	5.9	6.5	6.1	6.4	6.8
Malaysia	1.0	1.6	3.1	3.8	3.7	3.9	4.4	5.5
China	1.2	1.4	2.0	2.7	3.2	3.0	3.4	3.8
India	2.2	2.7	2.4	3.1	2.7	3.0	3.5	3.1
USSR	2.8	3.0	2.6	2.7	2.8	2.7	2.5	2.9
Brazil	0.8	1.4	2.9	2.7	2.7	2.6	3.0	2.6
Argentina	0.6	0.6	0.9	1.3	1.6	1.7	2.1	2.3
World	26.4	31.9	39.2	41.7	43.3	42.6	46.3	49.4

Source: See table 3.1.
a. Major oilseeds include soybean, cottonseed, peanut, sunflower, rapeseed, flaxseed, copra, and palm kernel. Major oilmeals include soybean, cottonseed, rapeseed, sunflower, fish, peanut, copra, linseed, palm kernel. Major vegetable and marine oils include soybean, palm, sunflower, rapeseed, cottonseed, peanut, coconut, olive, fish, palm kernel, linseed.
b. 1985/86 figures are preliminary.

TABLE 3.13 **World trade in major oilseeds**[a]
(thousand metric tons)

	1972/73	1975/76	1980/81	1981/82	1982/83	1983/84	1984/85	1985/86[b]
Exports								
United States	13,723	15,689	21,568	27,142	26,318	21,642	17,720	20,994
Argentina	2	112	2,290	2,235	1,460	3,405	3,460	3,240
EC-12[c]	611	557	1,112	1,228	1,720	1,616	2,138	2,736
France	260	158	622	626	1,063	1,030	1,179	1,561
Canada	1,791	907	2,157	1,971	1,863	2,217	2,193	2,267
China	352	222	568	335	592	1,059	1,361	1,593
Brazil	1,866	3,358	1,539	824	1,329	1,592	3,477	1,213
Imports								
EC-12[c]	10,999	14,382	16,970	19,419	19,213	16,438	16,864	17,622
Germany (FR)	3,637	4,515	4,743	5,087	5,068	3,856	4,670	4,948
Netherlands	1,682	2,198	3,382	3,589	3,592	3,472	3,587	3,328
Spain	923	2,002	2,829	3,383	3,163	2,710	1,981	2,174
Japan	4,831	4,684	5,725	6,038	6,444	6,297	6,486	6,578
USSR	772	1,833	1,464	1,557	1,127	1,025	942	1,995
Taiwan	652	800	1,081	1,194	1,283	1,366	1,480	1,632
Mexico	77	227	1,755	1,241	1,556	1,964	2,222	1,454
South Korea	88	168	575	589	731	728	840	1,030
World[c]	21,197	24,223	31,471	36,078	35,096	33,126	32,478	34,078

Source: See table 3.1.
a. Major oilseeds include soybean, cottonseed, peanut, sunflower, rapeseed, flaxseed, copra, and palm kernel.
b. 1985/86 figures are preliminary.
c. Figures include intra-EC trade.

T A B L E 3.14   **World trade in major oilmeals**[a]
(thousand metric tons)

	1972/73	1975/76	1980/81	1981/82	1982/83	1983/84	1984/85	1985/86[b]
Exports								
Brazil	1,560	4,169	8,657	7,961	8,220	7,814	8,825	7,137
EC-12[c]	3,052	2,918	5,118	5,837	7,291	6,934	7,079	7,024
Germany (FR)	1,477	1,010	1,707	2,199	2,544	2,046	2,346	2,764
Netherlands	663	780	1,934	1,757	2,292	2,029	1,960	1,864
United States	4,502	4,847	6,404	6,507	6,592	5,019	4,564	5,602
Argentina	688	970	1,534	2,354	3,299	4,026	4,257	4,952
China	0	16	208	299	786	1,141	1,077	1,484
Chile	27	221	456	771	755	781	1,113	1,185
India	1,223	1,460	961	985	923	835	800	915
Imports								
EC-12[c]	9,868	11,344	14,706	17,341	18,092	17,733	19,979	20,699
Germany (FR)	2,898	2,776	3,491	4,314	4,395	4,284	4,585	4,818
France	1,756	2,349	3,259	3,695	3,570	3,705	3,627	4,124
Netherlands	1,062	1,489	2,204	2,391	3,119	2,606	3,546	3,362
Denmark	899	1,183	2,057	2,049	2,031	1,911	1,908	2,254
United Kingdom	1,090	906	974	1,413	1,639	1,709	1,903	1,691
Germany (DR)	733	961	938	1,294	1,297	1,526	1,285	1,335
Poland	812	1,006	1,462	945	596	965	1,023	1,187
World[c]	14,570	18,671	26,940	28,819	31,521	30,154	32,171	33,296

Source: See table 3.1.
a. Major oilmeals include soybean, cottonseed, rapeseed, sunflowerseed, fish, peanut, copra, linseed, palm kernel.
b. 1985/86 figures are preliminary.
c. Figures include intra-EC trade.

TABLE 3.15   **World trade in major vegetable and marine oils**[a]
(million metric tons)

	1972/73	1975/76	1980/81	1981/82	1982/83	1983/84	1984/85	1985/86[b]
Exports								
Malaysia	896	1,489	2,764	3,054	3,361	3,266	3,740	4,707
EC-12[c]	1,522	1,836	2,742	2,915	3,091	3,346	3,544	3,706
Germany (FR)	360	551	713	773	774	724	850	963
Argentina	283	279	518	878	1,224	1,320	1,639	1,848
Philippines	429	851	1,047	949	1,029	586	657	1,240
United States	1,055	883	1,527	1,574	1,597	1,376	1,235	1,122
Imports								
EC-12[c]	3,150	3,119	3,498	4,043	4,205	4,093	4,396	4,716
Germany (FR)	725	592	855	903	956	1,016	997	1,074
United Kingdom	731	659	592	746	744	750	836	909
India	191	150	1,311	963	1,263	1,697	1,357	1,184
United States	587	1,021	777	670	700	727	788	1,110
Pakistan	64	240	455	573	663	630	644	984
Singapore	282	236	560	599	518	882	1,171	941
World[c]	6,707	8,439	12,596	13,520	14,353	14,415	16,446	16,983

Source: See table 3.1.
a. Major vegetable and marine oils include soybean, palm, sunflowerseed, rapeseed, cottonseed, peanut, coconut, olive, fish, palm kernel, linseed.
b. 1985/86 figures are preliminary.
c. Figures include intra-EC trade.

TABLE 3.16   **Dairy production**
(thousand metric tons)

	1970	1975	1980	1981
Cow milk production				
EC-12	91,124	97,975	111,366	111,580
France	22,963	24,855	26,859	26,795
Germany (FR)	21,856	21,604	24,778	24,858
USSR	83,016	90,800	90,900	88,874
United States	53,054	52,344	58,298	60,223
India	7,630	9,600	13,500	14,000
Brazil	6,492	8,849	10,265	10,500
World	334,105	359,104	391,077	389,656
Butter production				
EC-12	1,562	1,741	1,981	1,936
France	483	556	618	599
Germany (FR)	505	521	578	545
USSR	963	1,231	1,388	1,318
India	428	551	588	620
United States	519	445	519	557
Germany (DR)	220	270	280	281
World	5,065	5,633	6,181	6,062
Cheese production				
EC-12	2,491	2,885	3,461	3,571
France	781	947	1,146	1,168
Italy	466	501	615	610
Netherlands	278	375	443	465
United States	998	1,275	1,807	1,940
USSR	478	559	648	656
Germany (DR)	149	184	210	211
Argentina	162	226	245	226
Brazil	120	173	200	217
World	5,388	6,448	8,032	8,284
Nonfat dry milk production				
EC-12	1,354	1,923	2,082	2,061
France	642	759	710	705
Germany (FR)	344	523	727	604
United Kingdom	94	105	237	251
United States	655	451	526	596
USSR	208	316	130	156
New Zealand	112	244	172	181
Japan	70	76	127	127
World	2,958	3,806	3,632	3,753

Note: Figures are from Foreign Agricultural Service data on 38 countries; 1986 figures are preliminary.
Source: See table 3.1.

1982	1983	1984	1985	1986
113,995	118,185	116,156	114,613	115,416
27,358	27,905	27,595	26,830	27,100
25,465	26,913	26,151	25,674	26,200
91,044	96,450	97,906	98,608	101,000
61,464	63,354	61,439	65,166	65,800
14,900	16,000	17,100	19,000	20,100
10,100	10,700	10,800	10,400	9,800
396,903	412,462	413,038	417,934	423,207
2,075	2,285	2,115	2,013	2,147
624	637	621	595	630
556	627	572	515	560
1,403	1,562	1,588	1,596	1,630
650	670	690	700	720
570	589	500	585	540
266	291	309	316	317
6,361	6,890	6,770	6,756	6,871
3,683	3,749	3,896	3,962	3,991
1,200	1,245	1,287	1,300	1,300
645	656	661	684	690
481	485	515	522	532
2,060	2,186	2,120	2,279	2,365
699	744	780	809	825
223	225	237	246	250
229	209	210	220	245
220	200	200	205	185
8,713	8,976	9,134	9,444	9,708
2,192	2,515	2,138	1,946	2,162
718	815	773	650	700
552	727	604	552	640
296	303	250	252	270
635	680	526	631	585
182	208	234	260	280
200	189	248	242	215
131	154	155	181	190
4,056	4,503	4,121	4,041	4,142

TABLE 3.17   **World butter trade**[a]
(thousand metric tons)

	1970	1975	1980	1981	1982	1983	1984	1985	1986
Exports									
EC-12[b]	497	59	507	420	348	278	304	304	259
France	110	78	178	176	136	117	168	188	105
Netherlands	46	170	183	201	218	193	189	165	150
Belgium/Luxembourg	51	73	162	152	166	118	146	157	150
Ireland	46	53	90	81	80	82	119	105	90
New Zealand	198	164	231	200	228	234	201	227	223
Germany (DR)	0	0	35	36	36	40	40	50	55
United States	4	1	0	54	68	34	51	48	25
Australia	103	35	24	16	7	17	44	47	49
Imports									
USSR	2	12	249	215	151	203	198	276	250
EC-12[b]	546	131	110	120	130	112	99	89	81
United Kingdom	395	484	204	210	185	184	161	141	150
Belgium/Luxembourg	40	70	124	143	165	111	120	139	123
Germany (FR)	49	28	40	59	56	64	74	100	95
Italy	38	54	44	52	51	47	50	65	60
World[b]	943	335	855	790	769	722	748	771	696
World[c]	943	894	1,352	1,343	1,312	1,197	1,244	1,259	1,227

Source: See table 3.1.
a. Figures are from Foreign Agricultural Service data on 38 countries. The 1986 figures are preliminary.
b. Excludes intra-EC trade data for the EC-6 in 1970–72, the EC-9 in 1973–80, the EC-10 in 1981–85, and the EC-12 since 1986.
c. Total includes intra-EC trade.

TABLE 3.18 **World cheese trade**[a]
(thousand metric tons)

	1970	1975	1980	1981	1982	1983	1984	1985	1986
Exports									
EC-12[b]	446	145	316	335	354	353	446	384	388
Netherlands	173	226	275	308	317	326	339	356	365
Germany (FR)	52	105	163	187	196	202	280	280	315
France	98	154	232	223	222	229	239	248	239
Denmark	66	100	173	187	198	203	243	201	206
New Zealand	91	65	69	80	81	75	96	85	98
Australia	41	34	61	54	57	54	55	68	66
Switzerland	47	54	64	65	63	63	64	66	66
Austria	21	31	41	43	43	41	46	42	37
Imports									
EC-12[b]	460	170	121	121	122	126	128	139	103
Italy	93	156	217	232	267	254	268	315	290
Germany (FR)	148	179	216	231	233	247	257	275	285
United Kingdom	155	152	116	140	130	134	145	161	170
Belgium/Luxembourg	48	66	92	91	91	96	112	91	92
United States	73	81	105	112	122	130	139	137	138
Japan	34	48	75	71	74	72	79	82	88
Australia	7	8	12	13	17	20	22	22	20
Canada	14	22	20	19	20	21	23	21	20
World[b]	743	452	710	721	757	754	872	822	829
World[c]	749	997	1,357	1,427	1,484	1,502	1,701	1,698	1,737

Source: See table 3.1.

a. Figures are from Foreign Agricultural Service data on 38 countries. The 1986 figures are preliminary.

b. Excludes intra-EC trade for the EC-6 in 1970–72, the EC-9 in 1973–80, the EC-10 in 1981–85, and the EC-12 since 1986.

c. Total includes intra-EC trade.

TABLE 3.19   **World nonfat dry milk trade**[a]
(thousand metric tons)

	1970	1975	1980	1981	1982	1983	1984	1985	1986
Exports									
United States	196	54	131	155	144	289	295	380	400
EC-12[b]	599	145	580	436	342	216	314	314	205
Germany (FR)	155	149	532	340	382	546	592	471	350
Ireland	31	108	130	123	80	87	208	201	124
France	284	119	138	135	113	260	257	191	260
New Zealand	158	141	172	163	135	223	235	235	216
Australia	53	67	13	7	29	37	61	93	82
Canada	135	42	60	62	119	82	70	61	50
Imports									
Mexico	36	14	176	149	97	122	100	145	161
Japan	61	44	102	83	93	92	90	104	90
USSR	20	23	70	77	90	47	57	60	50
EC-12[b]	390	18	32	20	22	20	21	27	37
Netherlands	108	146	202	173	233	407	481	393	250
Italy	160	160	274	159	212	267	292	256	240
Germany (FR)	4	2	50	80	157	249	169	153	310
South America	42	46	117	53	49	90	80	72	176
World[b]	1,153	508	1,019	875	832	972	1,108	1,198	1,048
World[c]	1,153	910	1,625	1,402	1,513	2,034	2,258	2,112	1,980

Source: See table 3.1.

a. Figures for 1986 are preliminary. Figures are from Foreign Agricultural Service data on 38 countries.

b. Excludes intra-EC trade data for the EC-6 in 1970–72, the EC-9 in 1973–80, the EC-10 in 1981–85, and the EC-12 since 1986.

c. Total includes intra-EC trade.

TABLE 3.20   **Beef and veal production**[a]
(thousand metric tons)

	1970	1975	1980	1981	1982	1983	1984	1985	1986
United States	10,103	11,271	9,999	10,353	10,425	10,748	10,928	10,996	11,082
EC-12	6,435	7,277	7,651	7,468	7,144	7,380	7,900	7,840	7,739
France	1,565	1,746	1,836	1,834	1,698	1,764	1,936	1,845	1,805
USSR	5,015	6,409	6,645	6,627	6,618	7,011	7,244	7,400	7,600
Argentina	2,624	2,439	2,822	2,929	2,579	2,384	2,558	2,740	2,740
Brazil	1,845	150	2,150	2,250	2,400	2,400	2,300	2,400	2,200
World	34,210	41,099	41,325	41,526	41,588	41,123	41,868	42,866	42,645

Source: See table 3.1.
a. Figures are in carcass weight equivalent for calendar years. The 1986 figures are preliminary.

TABLE 3.21   **World beef and veal trade[a]**
(thousand metric tons)

	1970	1975	1980	1981	1982	1983	1984	1985	1986
Exports									
EC-12[b]	c	364	569	602	420	498	761	772	839
EC-12[d]	614	1,281	1,758	1,762	1,565	1,715	1,968	2,045	2,180
Germany (FR)	61	142	354	388	345	358	448	436	480
France	137	337	309	351	346	329	400	430	437
Ireland	160	327	382	258	243	272	242	308	400
Australia	510	777	883	711	942	767	616	690	710
Brazil	124	101	169	279	357	400	480	530	430
New Zealand	272	305	346	347	366	372	287	332	253
Argentina	715	262	469	486	522	415	250	260	220
Uruguay	167	113	117	173	169	225	131	120	140
Imports									
United States	824	808	946	799	888	885	838	947	974
EC-12[b]	c	435	421	330	451	366	338	464	418
EC-12[d]	1,315	1,271	1,630	1,500	1,558	1,634	1,589	1,714	1,730
Italy	299	329	366	378	453	453	458	493	460
France	83	167	263	246	260	283	279	320	362
Germany (FR)	232	232	288	256	245	258	285	301	265
USSR	60	331	385	452	439	529	541	320	300
Japan	33	64	174	174	174	196	208	216	225
World[d]	2,900	3,327	4,481	4,551	4,720	4,600	4,607	4,868	4,818
World[b]	c	2,380	3,265	3,368	3,547	3,383	3,300	3,595	3,477

Source: See table 3.1.
a. Figures in carcass weight equivalent for calendar years. The 1986 figures are preliminary.
b. Figures exclude intra-EC trade. The EC intra-trade data excluded are for the EC-9 in 1973–80, the EC-10 in 1981–85, and the EC-12 since 1986.
c. Intra-EC trade data not available.
d. Figures include intra-EC trade.

TABLE 3.22 **Market share of beef and veal exports**[a]
(percentage)

	1970	1975	1980	1981	1982	1983	1984	1985	1986
Australia	17.6	23.4	19.7	15.6	20.0	16.7	13.7	14.2	14.7
Germany (FR)	2.1	4.3	7.9	8.5	7.3	7.8	9.9	9.0	10.0
France	4.7	10.1	6.9	7.7	7.3	7.2	8.9	8.8	9.1
Brazil	4.3	3.0	3.8	6.1	7.6	8.7	10.7	10.9	8.9
New Zealand	9.4	9.2	7.7	7.6	7.8	8.1	6.4	6.8	5.3
Argentina	24.7	7.9	10.5	10.7	11.1	9.0	5.6	5.3	4.6
Uruguay	5.7	3.4	2.6	3.8	3.6	4.9	2.9	2.5	2.9
EC-12	21.2	38.5	39.2	38.7	33.2	37.3	43.7	42.0	45.2

a. Market shares calculated using figures that include intra-EC trade (see table 3.21).

TABLE 3.23 **Pork production**[a]
(thousand metric tons)

	1970	1975	1980	1981	1982	1983	1984	1985	1986
China	0	7,094	11,341	11,884	12,718	13,161	14,447	16,547	17,000
EC-12	7,595	8,555	10,402	10,656	10,707	10,995	11,100	11,187	11,495
Germany (FR)	2,214	2,379	2,720	2,691	2,666	2,725	2,734	2,753	2,820
France	1,250	1,470	1,597	1,640	1,610	1,624	1,625	1,607	1,622
United States	6,667	5,343	7,537	7,199	6,454	6,894	6,719	6,716	6,389
USSR	3,194	5,651	5,183	5,220	5,265	5,760	5,927	5,900	5,850
World	25,352	38,859	48,902	48,951	49,254	50,693	51,633	54,066	54,736

Source: See table 3.1.
a. Figures are in carcass weight equivalent for calendar years. The 1986 figures are preliminary.

T A B L E 3.24   **World pork trade**[a]

(thousand metric tons)

	1970	1975	1980	1981	1982	1983	1984	1985	1986
Exports									
EC-12[b]	[c]	329	307	326	222	296	385	413	377
EC-12[d]	1,160	1,338	1,791	1,940	1,870	2,073	2,187	2,207	2,399
Netherlands	336	443	602	657	650	705	769	837	890
Denmark	523	546	683	729	738	774	776	793	850
Belgium/Luxembourg	163	234	277	299	224	280	285	250	297
China	0	94	160	166	230	248	273	263	292
Germany (DR)	20	35	209	272	210	210	210	210	210
Canada	33	41	118	129	163	158	175	196	215
Hungary	19	53	92	95	118	125	220	150	120
Imports									
EC-12[b]	[c]	527	179	125	129	122	138	147	93
EC-12[d]	1,125	1,394	1,694	1,659	1,822	1,907	1,936	1,998	2,055
Germany (FR)	138	333	424	447	464	499	489	515	480
United Kingdom	639	491	534	506	565	550	560	500	505
Italy	106	240	344	298	356	365	350	436	465
France	197	219	289	287	311	335	368	373	425
United States	223	199	249	245	278	318	433	512	490
Japan	24	178	155	262	202	238	279	272	280
USSR	16	46	120	115	115	100	120	246	250
Hong Kong	—	10	180	188	207	214	206	217	225
World[d]	1,562	1,995	2,782	3,046	2,996	3,292	3,537	3,547	3,749
World[b]	[c]	1,114	1,295	1,426	1,333	1,515	1,735	1,753	1,727

Source: See table 3.1.

a. Figures in carcass weight equivalent for calendar years. The 1986 figures are preliminary.
b. Figures exclude intra-EC trade. Data excluded are for the EC-9 in 1973–80, the EC-10 in 1981–85, and the EC-12 since 1986.
c. Intra-EC trade data not available.
d. Figures include intra-EC trade.

TABLE 3.25   **Market share of pork exports**[a]
(percentage)

	1970	1975	1980	1981	1982	1983	1984	1985	1986
Netherlands	21.5	22.2	21.6	21.6	21.7	21.4	21.7	23.6	23.7
Denmark	33.5	27.4	24.6	23.9	24.6	23.5	21.9	22.4	22.7
Belgium/Luxembourg	10.4	11.7	10.0	9.8	7.5	8.5	8.1	7.0	7.9
China	0.0	4.7	5.8	5.4	7.7	7.5	7.7	7.4	7.8
Germany (DR)	1.3	1.8	7.5	8.9	7.0	6.4	5.9	5.9	5.6
EC-12	74.3	67.1	64.4	63.7	62.4	63.0	61.8	62.2	64.0

Source: See table 3.1.
a. Market shares calculated using figures that include intra-EC trade (see table 3.24).

TABLE 3.26   **Poultry production**[a]
(thousand metric tons)

	1970	1975	1980	1981	1982	1983	1984	1985	1986
United States	4,651	4,845	6,596	6,949	7,000	7,151	7,427	7,865	8,346
EC-12	3,272	3,966	4,907	5,196	5,371	5,268	5,219	5,312	5,417
France	637	823	1,122	1,236	1,330	1,284	1,247	1,272	1,303
USSR	1,071	1,539	2,139	2,255	2,425	2,596	2,686	2,700	2,750
Brazil	245	434	1,326	1,491	1,596	1,580	1,398	1,530	1,650
Japan	490	756	1,154	1,134	1,209	1,257	1,309	1,395	1,399
World	12,015	15,548	22,236	23,401	24,297	23,534	24,240	25,165	26,097

Source: See table 3.1.
a. Data are on calendar year, in ready to cook equivalent. The 1986 figures are preliminary.

T A B L E 3.27   **World poultry trade**[a]
(thousand metric tons)

	1970	1975	1980	1981	1982	1983	1984	1985	1986
Exports									
EC-12[b]	c	149	339	479	455	457	385	346	305
EC-12[d]	342	421	679	830	826	839	774	775	758
France	29	92	252	358	363	399	343	324	295
Netherlands	222	232	272	304	289	283	272	277	280
Brazil	0	9	170	295	302	289	281	274	251
United States	62	95	316	375	261	225	209	211	257
Hungary	56	104	135	157	179	186	162	156	180
Imports									
EC-12[b]	c	99	80	79	67	82	101	119	89
EC-12[d]	289	358	389	384	410	435	460	495	484
Germany (FR)	258	292	276	269	277	252	254	261	263
USSR	61	50	159	253	260	206	114	141	140
Hong Kong	22	30	86	88	92	88	94	114	131
Japan	11	21	72	98	106	105	107	104	126
Saudi Arabia	0	37	194	182	209	227	156	180	125
World[d]	515	712	1,455	1,862	1,780	1,684	1,602	1,608	1,648
World[b]	c	440	1,096	1,484	1,370	1,302	1,213	1,179	1,195

Source: See table 3.1.
a. Data are on calendar year, in ready to cook equivalent. The 1986 figures are preliminary.
b. Figures for EC exclude intra-EC trade. The EC intra-trade data excluded are for the EC-9 in 1973–80, the EC-10 in 1981–85, and the EC-12 since 1986.
c. Intra-EC trade data not available.
d. Figures include intra-EC trade.

TABLE 3.28   **Market share of poultry exports**[a]
(percentage)

	1970	1975	1980	1981	1982	1983	1984	1985	1986
France	5.6	12.9	17.3	19.2	20.4	23.7	21.4	20.1	17.9
Netherlands	43.1	32.6	18.7	16.3	16.2	16.8	17.0	17.2	17.0
United States	12.0	13.3	21.7	20.1	14.7	13.4	13.4	13.0	15.6
Brazil	0.0	1.3	11.7	15.8	17.0	17.2	17.5	17.0	15.2
Hungary	10.9	14.6	9.3	8.4	10.1	11.0	10.1	9.7	10.9
EC-12	66.4	59.1	46.7	44.6	46.4	49.8	48.3	48.2	46.0

a. Market shares calculated using figures that include intra-EC trade (see table 3.27).

TABLE 3.29   **Sugar production**[a]
(thousand metric tons, raw value)

	1970/71	1975/76	1980/81	1981/82	1982/83	1983/84	1984/85	1985/86[b]
EC-12	9,854	11,398	14,003	17,129	15,989	13,287	14,424	14,437
USSR	8,983	8,093	7,174	6,413	7,392	8,700	8,587	8,250
Brazil	5,117	6,200	8,547	8,393	9,300	9,400	9,300	8,200
India[c]	4,501	5,612	6,542	9,727	9,508	7,042	7,071	7,983
Cuba	6,010	6,279	7,542	8,207	7,200	8,330	8,100	7,100
China	2,096	2,311	3,220	3,650	4,132	3,825	4,627	5,535
World	69,830	82,519	88,691	100,616	101,254	96,542	100,183	98,079

Source: See table 3.1.

a. Crop year is September/October, but includes the outturn of several Southern Hemisphere countries that begin sugar harvests prior to September. Brazil, Cuba, and India production figures are for sugarcane production.

b. The 1985/86 production figures are preliminary.

c. Includes Khandsai sugar (native type, semiwhite centrifugal sugar).

TABLE 3.30   **World sugar trade**[a]
(thousand metric tons)

	1970/71	1975/76	1980/81	1981/82	1982/83	1983/84	1984/85
Exports							
Cuba	6,906	5,731	6,668	7,734	6,792	7,000	7,100
EC-12[b]	1,926	3,374	5,952	5,797	6,714	5,962	5,677
France	800	1,610	2,908	3,225	3,066	3,250	2,500
Brazil	1,126	1,243	2,305	2,984	2,984	2,638	2,800
Australia	1,389	2,114	2,655	2,620	2,687	2,600	2,696
Thailand	57	486	847	2,419	1,393	1,379	1,600
Imports							
USSR	3,005	3,720	4,898	6,883	5,926	5,600	5,300
EC-12[b]	3,732	4,050	2,426	2,686	2,542	3,115	2,734
United Kingdom	2,211	2,351	1,327	1,307	1,050	1,500	1,400
United States	4,711	3,664	3,746	3,494	2,583	2,916	2,200
Japan	2,600	2,345	1,612	2,209	1,770	1,908	1,787
China	530	525	975	1,060	2,480	1,121	1,000
World[b]	22,064	22,850	28,975	32,977	31,590	29,996	29,538

Source: See table 3.1.
a. Data from Foreign Agricultural Service on trade for individual countries is available only through 1984/85.
b. Figures include intra-EC trade.

TABLE 3.31   **Cotton production**
(thousand 480-pound bales)

	1970/71	1975/76	1980/81	1981/82	1982/83	1983/84	1984/85	1985/86[a]
China	10,500	10,900	12,400	13,600	16,500	21,300	28,700	19,000
United States	10,192	8,302	11,122	15,646	11,963	7,771	12,982	13,432
USSR	10,770	11,610	13,498	13,277	11,932	12,065	11,876	12,095
India	4,671	5,440	6,319	6,807	7,004	6,086	7,925	8,400
Pakistan	2,500	2,269	3,300	3,494	3,781	2,188	4,628	5,669
World	55,306	54,201	64,989	71,189	68,060	67,663	88,132	78,947

Source: See table 3.1.
a. The 1985/86 figures are preliminary.

TABLE 3.32   **World cotton trade**
(thousand 480-pound bales)

	1970/71	1975/76	1980/81	1981/82	1982/83	1983/84	1984/85	1985/86[a]
Exports								
Pakistan	473	418	1,490	1,097	1,273	377	1,171	3,148
USSR	2,450	3,890	4,070	4,295	3,890	3,202	3,200	3,000
China	100	250	6	0	75	800	1,200	2,900
United States	3,897	3,311	5,926	6,567	5,207	6,786	6,215	1,960
Australia	19	69	243	371	617	374	575	1,132
Imports								
EC-12[b]	5,037	4,971	3,924	4,283	4,643	4,678	4,807	4,645
Japan	3,669	3,220	3,207	3,504	3,137	3,338	3,125	3,054
South Korea	557	1,013	1,527	1,496	1,562	1,602	1,601	1,682
Taiwan	735	1,024	965	1,135	1,044	1,171	1,294	1,534
Italy	816	886	870	1,001	1,078	1,150	1,162	1,185
Hong Kong	833	1,321	708	699	780	997	851	1,096
World	17,748	19,093	19,711	20,208	19,441	19,227	20,285	20,278
Market share of exports (percentage)								
Pakistan	2.7	2.2	7.6	5.4	6.5	2.0	5.8	15.5
USSR	13.8	20.4	20.6	21.3	20.0	16.7	15.8	14.8
China	0.6	1.3	0.0	0.0	0.4	4.2	5.9	14.3
United States	22.0	17.3	30.1	32.5	26.8	35.3	30.6	9.7
Australia	0.1	0.4	1.2	1.8	3.2	1.9	2.8	5.6

Source: See table 3.1.
a. The 1985/86 figures are preliminary.
b. Figures include any intra-EC trade.

4 The Link Between Agricultural Policy and Trade Policy

In order to understand the driving economic and political forces behind the trade negotiations in agriculture, national agricultural programs and their relationship to trade have to be examined.

The point is often made that agriculture differs from other industries. These differences are used to justify national agricultural programs, and different treatment in the General Agreement on Tariffs and Trade (GATT) than is accorded other industries. In some West European countries, and in the United States, this difference was carried to the point of attributing superior moral and political values to tillers of the soil. The political imperative of ''saving the family farm'' has been a slogan of most major political parties in a number of developed countries. In developing countries, however, tillers of the soil are often called ''peasants,'' which is generally viewed as a derogatory term, and supporting a peasant way of life is rarely a political goal.

There are several economic characteristics unique to agriculture. One is that despite technological advances, the production of most agricultural products still is heavily influenced by the forces of nature—weather, sunlight, insects, and diseases.

Second, agricultural production (especially crop production) has a distinct cycle. Crops are planted at specific times and require a certain period of time to mature. In most cases this is a few months, but in the case of tree crops it is years. While plant breeding can alter the time span, these alterations do not change fixed cycles for any specific variety. In livestock production, the gestation period of the animal is unvaried and, thus, only the growing rates between birth and slaughter can be affected by science.

The fixed physical cycles result in a short-term supply response that is highly inelastic for most agricultural products because it is largely dependent upon decisions made at or before the time of planting or animal breeding.

Food, along with air and water, is essential for human life. However, unlike many other goods, there are physical limits on the total amount of

69

food an individual can consume in terms of bulk and, to some extent, calories. This translates into a highly inelastic total demand for food. There is, however, a relatively high elasticity for total caloric intake up to a certain level and for different foodstuffs. As populations grow more prosperous, there is a marked shift from basic food grains, roots, and tubers (rice, wheat, potatoes, coarse grains, etc.) to proteins (meat, fish, and poultry).

These characteristics of both low supply and demand elasticity in the short run lead to substantial and continuing price instability. Governments in both developed and developing countries have found that sharp rises in the prices of basic foodstuffs are unsettling to consumers, and few countries have been able to resist the political appeal of an adequate, stable supply of food at stable prices as a national policy.

Agriculture has certain characteristics that also affect longer run supply responses. An expansion of agricultural output requires:

● an expansion of land under cultivation, or

● new investment in output-increasing capital such as breeding animals, irrigation, tractors, or harvesting machines, or

● the development and adoption of new output-increasing technology such as new crop varieties or animal breeding practices.

Often, all three are involved. As a result of these factors, the long-run response to price increases is relatively slow—you cannot increase total agricultural output merely by adding another shift or setting up a new production line in an existing factory.

Moreover, most of the investment in agriculture, and most of its labor force, are industry specific. Once committed to the production of agricultural products, investment will continue in that production because the alternatives are virtually nonexistent. An irrigation system in Kansas or in the Punjab will be used to produce agricultural products even at very low prices because it cannot be used for any other purpose. And, since output-increasing technology also generally reduces cost, such technology will continue to be used even if agricultural prices fall very far.

These economic (and political) characteristics of agriculture have led to a web of governmental interventions in agriculture around the world. In socialist countries, of course, the major factors of production are state-owned and controlled, even though important elements of private-sector agricultural activity continue in most socialist economies. More important is the heavy government involvement in the agricultural industry in market economies, developed and developing.

This involvement is not new. A major portion of research to develop new agricultural technology has been supported for decades by public funds in Europe, the United States, Japan, and developing countries. A good share of agricultural investment, in every country, has been by governments that have built rural roads, electricity, telephones, credit systems, education systems, irrigation, and other infrastructure development programs for the agricultural sector and its rural inhabitants. There is virtually no agricultural enterprise in any economy touched by modernization and development that has not benefited by a host of government programs; the richer the economy, the greater the benefits are likely to have been.

In addition to these activities, there is a widespread series of direct governmental interventions in the pricing of agricultural products, generally in the name of price stabilization and to provide "fair" prices to producers. The exact form of these interventions varies, but they often include the use of direct government buying agencies (or marketing boards) for importing, exporting, or both. Policies include minimum prices and maximum prices.

Border measures to influence prices include import taxes, export taxes, variable levies, quotas, and state trading. In addition to these overt economic measures, there is a profusion of regulations, generally in the name of consumer health and safety, which may affect what can be traded. In developed countries these various government interventions generally raise agricultural product prices above prices in world trade and sustain output at higher levels than would otherwise be the case. Developing countries, on the other hand, more often have policy mechanisms that keep internal prices below traded prices in world markets, and as a result, they have retarded agricultural development and discouraged agricultural output.

Any governmental intervention that affects production, consumption, or trade in agricultural products distorts resource use and trade. As a practical matter, however, it is useful to distinguish between policies having a general effect and those having a significant trade effect. Almost all of the policies that attempt to maintain domestic prices significantly above or below world prices fall into the category of policies having trade effects. This holds true whether it is done by import barriers, state trading, or export subsidies. Policies that pay producers prices well above world prices without limiting production also have a trade effect.

The effects of policies maintained by major participants in the trading system are the focal point of the tensions in agricultural trade today. Therefore, an overview of the major policies will be given, then an evaluation of their impact upon trade will be developed.

The European Community

Mention was made earlier of the European and Japanese desire for self-sufficiency growing out of World War II. While it initially took different forms in Europe, the founding and enlargement of the European Community (EC), and the development of its common agricultural policy (CAP), institutionalized market-intervention policies long in place in countries such as Germany and France. However, the EC included Denmark, the Netherlands, and the United Kingdom, which previously had open markets for agricultural products.

The CAP began with three basic cornerstones:

- common prices for agricultural products in all member countries

- an absolute preference for EC producers over outside producers, and

- common funding of its agricultural programs through the EC Commission in Brussels.

Subsequent events have led to violations of two of these three basic principles.

There initially were, and still are, huge disparities in farm size, land productivity, and agricultural structure between EC countries. The necessity of achieving a common price meant that this price had to be high enough to satisfy the political needs of the high-cost producer countries. These prices, of course, were much higher than needed to cover the costs of the lower cost producers.

The policy instrument chosen to provide the market preference for national producers was the variable levy on most major agricultural products—grains, meat, poultry, and eggs. The levy is determined by the difference between the lowest world offer price for the commodity and a politically determined internal target price. Since these internal prices generally are fixed at a level above prevailing world market prices, an export restitution system was instituted that pays exporters the difference between high internal prices and world market prices for products sold outside the EC.

The policies were to be financed by the fees from the variable import levies, plus a fixed percentage of the value-added tax collected by the member governments. In the 1970s the EC was enlarged to take in the United Kingdom, Ireland, and Denmark; in 1981 Greece joined, and in 1986 Spain and Portugal. The enlargement of the EC increased disparities in farm structure by adding both new low-cost producers and new high-cost producers for nearly every product.

It should be remembered that when the CAP was being developed, the original six EC member countries were large net importers of most agricultural commodities. The CAP was conceived and designed as a policy that used trade measures as a mechanism to maintain and stabilize internal prices. As long as there was a net deficit in internal production relative to demand, the variable levy could effectively control internal prices. Of course, there was a problem of exporting final products depending upon agricultural raw materials, such as poultry and wheat flour, but this was dealt with by providing export subsidies to make up the difference between internal and external raw material prices.

While the effects of the variable levies are similar to the use of import quotas, the EC argued that variable levies were consistent with the GATT. Other countries had, and still have, a different view, but the levies exist as a political reality that must be dealt with.

The variable levies completely isolated EC producers (and consumers) from world market forces, but they were not especially disruptive to world trade for products in which the EC was a net importer as long as domestic market growth equaled or exceeded domestic production growth. Initially, the policies provided a major income transfer from EC consumers to EC producers through the internal price mechanism. In terms of direct public expenditures, the policies were relatively low cost. The EC was pleased with its policies in the early 1970s, when sharp world price increases for agricultural products disrupted more open economies. High world commodity prices in the 1970s made it inexpensive to finance the exports of surplus products. It was easy and costless (to budgets) to escalate internal prices sufficiently to maintain real price levels for agricultural producers at a time when world prices, in real terms, were declining.

A combination of price incentives from the CAP and widespread technological advance led to increased agricultural investment and domestic production increases at a time when the domestic demand for farm products was stagnant or falling. As we have seen, in less than a decade, the EC went from a major net importer to a net exporter of grains, sugar, meat, and poultry. As imports fell and exports rose, the direct budget costs of the CAP began to rise. Surpluses developed that were too large to be exported at a reasonable cost, and it became necessary to develop internal price-intervention mechanisms to buy and store excess production. Large stocks of grains, beef, butter, nonfat dry milk, wine, and olive oil were accumulated by intervention agencies that bought surpluses at fixed intervention prices. Not only were these stocks expensive to store, but internal prices fell below the border price as internal surpluses grew.

A significant gap in the protection provided by the CAP was caused by the binding of tariffs on oilseeds and oilseed products and on certain nongrain feedstuffs (which had taken place in the Dillon Round of trade negotiations in the early 1960s). As the internal price of feed wheat and coarse grains escalated, the importation and use of soybean meal, tapioca, corn gluten, and citrus pulp as substitutes for grains in feed rations grew rapidly.

The EC has acted to close this loophole in two ways. First, it initiated an oilseed support program that operates by providing farmers a target price for domestic oilseed and making very high payments to domestic processors for processing the oilseed acquired at the high internal price. This target price is, of course, well above the world market price. The program has resulted in a substantial expansion of harvested area of oilseeds and a huge increase in oilseed output. The processor payments are geared to ensure that the domestic meal and oil output displaces levy-free imports of foreign oilseeds and products.

In the case of the most important nongrain feed substitute, tapioca from Thailand, the EC pressured the Thais into a voluntary restraint agreement that cut EC imports of tapioca from 8.5 million to 5.5 million tons between 1984 and 1985. The EC has repeatedly suggested that it be allowed to put import controls on all grain substitutes, but the United States, which is the major supplier of soybeans and corn gluten feed, has vigorously resisted.

The EC Commission is continuing its efforts to limit nongrain feed substitutes. In February 1987 the Commission recommended that a hefty tax be placed on the consumption of all vegetable oils, with the proceeds used to finance the EC oilseeds policy. The United States and other oilseed and vegetable oil exporters have strongly opposed such a tax, and the United States has threatened to retaliate if it is imposed.

It also is widely reported in mid-1987 that a commodity group in the EC will file a countervailing duty complaint against imports of US corn gluten feed, basing it upon a recent Canadian government decision that US farm programs for corn represent countervailable subsidies. If successful, this could substantially increase the internal price of the feed substitute and reduce its use in EC feed rations.

As the agricultural production in the EC has exceeded domestic consumption, the cost of exporting the surplus has risen dramatically. This cost was held down when world market prices were strong and the dollar was strong relative to EC currencies. However, in 1985 and 1986, as the nominal price of agricultural products in US dollars fell in world markets and the US dollar fell relative to EC currencies, the cost of the CAP soared even further. Member states were required to increase the amount of their value-added tax (VAT) allocated to the EC budget from 1 percent to 1.4 percent in 1985. The soaring costs of exporting or storing the dairy surpluses led to the imposition of a mandatory supply control program in dairy in 1984, which provided for a very high tax on individual marketings above a specified base. This program halted output increases in dairy, and it even reduced output slightly; but since the total production quota was set well above domestic consumption, the EC is still the largest exporter of dairy products and the program costs are still increasing. In late 1986 the EC took action to further reduce dairy quotas by 9.5 percent over the next two years.

The impact of the shift from net import to net export status, and the decline of real prices in world markets, can be seen in the EC expenditures for price support programs shown in table 4.1. Costs for the major commodities discussed earlier increased roughly fourfold from 1970–72 to 1980–82 as the Community became an exporter of all of these products. These costs doubled again between 1980 and 1986. Moreover, some authorities argue that these statistics substantially underestimate the true budget costs because of overvaluation of accumulated surplus stocks which will eventually be sold at a big loss.

Rising surpluses, falling world commodity prices, and the falling US dollar brought the CAP to its fiscal limits in 1985.[1] In 1986 the EC Commission recommended modest cuts in some target prices as well as measures that would change the internal intervention mechanism in ways that would reduce prices received by producers of grains and beef.

Even so, spending on the CAP will exceed the EC's common resources, and responsibility for financing some agricultural programs is being shifted back to member states. This includes the financing of stockholding and, more recently, of income supplements to farmers.

1. The EC is not allowed by its member states to run a deficit. Thus, the fiscal limit for the CAP is technically the amount of revenue produced by the VAT and the variable levies.

TABLE 4.1   **EAGGF Guarantee expenditures, 1970–86[a]**

	Million units of account								
Product	1970	1971	1972	1973	1974	1975	1976	1977	1978
Cereals	894.4	473.6	908.2	1,029.5	399.8	620.8	655.9	629.9	1,112.5
Rice	50.6	49.8	50.4	11.4	1.2	4.2	18.4	13.5	17.9
Protein products[c]	—	—	—	—	3.6	11.1	15.4	13.8	42.6
Cotton	n.a.	n.a.	n.a.	n.a.	n.a.	n.a.	n.a.	n.a.	n.a.
Sugar	192.8	110.3	151.7	136.5	108.8	309.2	229.3	598.4	878.0
Oils and fats	281.2	113.0	335.8	368.7	141.0	231.4	309.0	305.0	324.8
Olive oil[d]	n.a.	n.a.	235.2	281.4	129.6	203.7	191.1	205.1	182.2
Oilseeds	n.a.	n.a.	95.3	84.5	10.3	25.4	85.7	82.5	142.5
Milk products	991.5	566.0	573.7	1,497.0	1,219.2	1,149.8	2,277.7	2,924.1	4,014.6
Eggs and poultry	16.5	11.9	11.8	23.3	16.9	8.4	15.1	25.6	38.1
Beef and veal	30.8	19.1	7.4	16.6	324.4	980.0	615.9	467.7	638.7
Pigmeat	43.4	52.3	49.5	96.7	66.5	53.8	29.0	37.3	45.0
Sheep and goatmeat	—	—	—	—	—	—	—	—	—
Subtotal	2,501.2	1,396.0	2,088.5	3,179.7	2,281.4	3,368.7	4,165.7	5,015.3	7,112.2
Fruits and vegetables	56.5	53.9	61.4	34.9	66.9	90.3	185.1	178.2	100.7
Wine	n.a.	28.2	57.7	12.4	41.9	139.1	133.8	89.9	63.7
Tobacco	5.0	73.8	88.5	129.6	183.6	228.5	185.4	205.2	216.1
Fishery products	n.a.	0.2	1.1	1.3	1.2	9.3	11.0	8.8	15.4
Other[e]	40.2	19.2	26.9	456.7	522.9	891.4	906.1	1,333.0	1,164.6
Grand total	2,602.9	1,571.3	2,329.2	3,814.6	3,097.9	4,727.4	5,587.1	6,830.4	8,672.7

EAGGF   European Agricultural Guidance and Guarantee Fund; — nil; n.a.   not available.
Source: Agricultural Situation Reports 1974–1986, Commision of EC, Brussels and Luxembourg.
a. The expenditure items are taken from the returns made by the member states under the advance payment system and are charged to a given financial year under Article 109 of the Financial Regulation.
b. Budget decided on 7 July 1986.
c. Protein products include peas, field beans, dried fodder. For 1974–1977 figures are only for dried fodder.
d. Includes intervention spending on colza, sunflower, rapeseed, flaxseed, and soybeans.
e. Includes seeds, hops, flax and hemp, non-annex II products as well as accession and monetary compensatory amounts in trade.

			Million European currency units				
1979	*1980*	*1981*	*1982*	*1983*	*1984*	*1985*	*1986*[b]
1,563.7	1,669.0	1,921.4	1,824.5	2,441.2	1,650.0	2,310.2	3,197.5
42.9	58.7	21.7	50.3	92.9	47.8	50.1	102.5
61.9	60.5	65.5	82.8	142.3	215.6	372.5	495.0
n.a.	n.a.	54.9	96.2	140.1	88.2	212.7	387.0
939.8	575.2	767.5	1,241.9	1,316.2	1,631.5	1,804.5	1,642.0
606.0	687.3	1,025.4	1,213.8	1,620.9	1,752.0	1,802.8	2,750.0
388.2	317.9	439.8	493.1	675.3	1,096.4	692.2	1,034.0
216.5	356.5	577.3	716.9	941.9	655.2	1,107.2	1,712.0
4,527.5	4,752.0	3,342.7	3,327.7	4,396.1	5,441.7	5,933.2	6,100.0
79.5	85.5	83.9	103.9	123.3	69.8	63.2	131.0
748.2	1,363.3	1,436.9	1,158.6	1,736.5	2,546.8	2,745.8	2,682.0
104.9	115.6	154.6	111.6	145.0	195.9	165.4	220.0
—	53.5	191.5	251.7	305.6	433.5	502.4	526.0
8,674.4	9,420.6	9,066.0	9,463.0	12,460.1	14,072.8	15,962.8	18,233.0
442.9	687.3	641.1	914.3	1,196.1	1,454.6	1,230.7	927.5
61.9	299.5	459.4	570.6	659.2	1,222.6	921.4	1,087.0
225.4	309.3	361.8	622.6	671.3	776.4	862.9	792.0
17.0	23.0	28.0	34.0	25.7	15.6	16.1	41.3
1,019.1	575.2	584.9	801.1	799.2	804.5	750.3	1,072.5
10,440.7	11,314.9	11,141.2	12,405.6	15,811.6	18,346.5	19,744.2	22,153.3

Despite rising internal pressures due to budget costs and rising external pressures because of trade disruptions, the basic political support for the CAP within the EC appears unshaken. Many Europeans believe the CAP is "the basic glue which holds the Common Market together." Moreover, the political system driving the CAP has, thus far, resisted both internal and external pressures for fundamental reform. Predictions of the early demise of the CAP, going back nearly two decades, have proven wrong and may well prove wrong again. Never before, however, as the world enters a new GATT round, have pressures within the Community for reform been as great as they are now.

The harsh reality is that the CAP is a policy based upon two assumptions that have proven wrong. The first assumption was that the EC would remain a net importer of many farm products, allowing the CAP to be operated and financed without resort to large-scale stock accumulation and ever-rising expenditures on export subsidies. The second assumption was that a rapidly expanding world market with stable or rising prices would keep the CAP low-cost and relatively undisruptive to world trade, even for products the EC exported. Stagnant domestic consumption and rapid increases in domestic agricultural productivity and output have invalidated the first assumption. World market conditions have made the second assumption wrong. As the dollar has fallen relative to EC currencies in 1986 and 1987, the cost of these false assumptions has risen sharply to a level where they cannot be ignored.

Japan

Differences in natural endowments and historical developments have led Japanese agricultural policy in a different direction than in most other industrial countries. Japan is a country with a limited land area relative to its population and relatively little arable land in its total land area. Thus, under any circumstances, the opportunities for extensive farm production are limited.

World War II and its aftermath left Japan with two important legacies regarding food and its production. First, the wartime food shortage left a lasting desire for self-sufficiency in the production of basic foodstuffs. In Japan, this is translated largely into self-sufficiency in rice. Second, the postwar constitution contained rules that inhibited the development of tenancy or land rental systems in Japan. Thus, the major consolidation of farm operations, which has occurred in other market economies in response to technical change and the expansion of nonfarm employment, was effectively blocked. Even though farm structures could not be easily adjusted, farm labor responded as industrial growth occurred. By the 1980s, about 85 percent of the income of farm families came from nonfarm employment, and only a small fraction (14.3 percent) of the people involved in agriculture were classified as full-time farmers.

Japanese agricultural policy has had as its objectives:

• minimum self-sufficiency

• maintaining farm income at levels comparable to nonfarmers.

The basic method of achieving these goals has been the use of import restrictions on final products, which result in internal prices at levels well above world prices. Rice, wheat, and barley are handled exclusively by a government agency that buys internal production directly from farmers and is responsible for all import purchases. Import quotas are applied to 22 agricultural items, the most important being beef. Agricultural raw materials, such as feedgrain and soybeans, are imported freely; import restrictions apply largely to final products or specialty products.

Japanese farms are small by world standards and average only 1.2 hectares per farm household. Most are modern, however, and have very high yields. Rice still dominates domestic agricultural production and policy. It is the only crop on nearly half the farms in Japan and accounts for one-third of farm income.

With the rapid growth of Japanese consumer incomes, significant changes occurred in consumption patterns and, as a result, in import patterns. Rice consumption per capita peaked in 1962, and by 1984 was less than two-thirds the peak level. Wheat consumption increased, as did the consumption of red meat, poultry, and fruits and vegetables.

Japan has been self-sufficient in rice for some time. In fact, in the late 1970s, it accumulated a substantial rice surplus, which was subsidized into export markets and into animal feed use. The United States charged Japan with unfair trade practices in 1980 and an agreement was negotiated limiting Japan's exports. Policies to bring a downward adjustment in rice production have been in effect since 1969. Similar programs reduce output of oranges and several other crops. Japan now has a milk surplus.

Food self-sufficiency has declined steadily in Japan. Even though Japan remains self-sufficient in rice, its total self-sufficiency in grains is 32 percent, in beef 70 percent, and in pork 85 percent. In terms of calories consumed, only 52 percent of the Japanese food intake comes from domestic production.

Japanese agricultural interests have strongly resisted the importation of products that can be produced in Japan. They have supported the open imports of feed grains and soybeans, crucial to their poultry and livestock production, but they have bitterly opposed the liberalization of such items as beef, citrus, and dairy products that directly compete with high-cost Japanese production. The views of Japanese agricultural interests are important to Japanese trade policy because of the disproportionate weight of rural voters in the Japanese Diet, and the heavy dependence of the ruling Liberal Democratic Party upon agricultural support in elections.

The Japanese system of import barriers has maintained protection for its agricultural producers primarily by allowing high consumer prices. The direct budget costs of maintaining this system have been relatively low, and come largely from subsidizing consumer prices for rice to levels below producer prices.

Apart from the short-lived rice exports, the Japanese policy has not directly affected markets outside Japan. During the period of rising world prices and agricultural trade, the Japanese were relatively free from outside pressures to change their system. Two factors sharply changed this, however. One was the steadily rising Japanese current account surplus, including its huge bilateral surpluses with the United States. This has led to increasing political pressure for the Japanese to allow greater market access for all imports, including agricultural imports, in order to balance their access to foreign manufactured-product markets. As world trade in agricultural and commodity prices fell, this pressure was intensified by lower cost agricultural exporters interested in greater access to the affluent consumer market in Japan. Therefore, whereas US and EC domestic policies have run into trouble over domestic budget costs, Japanese agricultural policies are under pressure from external political forces.

Recently, internal conflicts over agricultural policy also have arisen in Japan. The steadily rising costs of the rice policies led to a major confrontation between the government and farm organizations in 1986 and major reforms in the rice program are being discussed. The action of US rice growers who filed a complaint charging that Japanese rice policies were an unfair trade practice serves to highlight Japanese prices relative to world prices.

The rising value of the yen and the high Japanese trade surplus with the United States and the world has brought further world examination of Japan's internal policies. There is general agreement that more of Japan's economic activities should be aimed toward expanding domestic consumption—including cuts in the high cost of food and the high cost of land, which reduces the scope for expanding housing. Both domestic food costs and high land costs are related to the restrictive agricultural import policies in Japan. Thus, for the first time in postwar history, Japanese agricultural policy appears to conflict with national economic policy. By April 1987, a combination of internal and external pressures led Japanese leaders to agree to bring their agricultural policies into the GATT negotiations.

The United States

US agricultural policies have their roots in the Great Depression of the 1930s, which brought the first large-scale government intervention into the production and marketing of agricultural products.

The collapse of farm prices of the 1930s brought federal government intervention to US agricultural markets. Three concepts were born that persist fifty years later. One was the concept of price supports, whereby the government stands ready to make nonrecourse loans to eligible farmers for crops at a specified minimum price. Price support loans can be repaid by forfeiting the crop to the government if the product's market price is not high enough to allow the farmer to sell the product for enough to repay the loan. The second concept, initiated in the 1933 legislation, involved production controls on basic crops, usually carried out by requiring the producer to reduce the harvested acreage of the crops concerned. A third element, begun in legislation of 1938, was the use of deficiency payments to make up the difference between the market price and some "target price" determined to be desirable.

US agricultural support policy has centered on these three concepts for a half century. From the beginning, basic field crops were the objects of support—wheat, corn, cotton, rice, peanuts, and tobacco. Dairy price supports were added later, with a program of direct purchases of manufactured dairy products used to maintain a minimum price for milk used in manufacturing. There has never been any permanent direct market intervention for beef, pork, or poultry, nor for minor field crops, fruit, or vegetables.

During World War II, the price support level for these commodities was tied to an automatic escalator relating to farm input prices (not costs). At the end of World War II, these high price supports were continued and, by the mid-1950s, US domestic prices on most supported commodities were above world prices. US exports fell, and government stocks of surplus commodities rose. The US resorted to the use of export subsidies to compete in world markets, and of import quotas on several agricultural products. The need for the latter to maintain domestic programs caused the United States to seek and obtain a GATT waiver relieving it of obligations regarding import quotas.

In the 1960s the fundamental mix of US policy was changed. Domestic price support levels for the basic field crops were cut drastically. Deficiency payments were used to maintain farm income, and large-scale land retirement was used to control output. The need for export subsidies was eliminated for some crops, and reduced sharply for most others.

The relative mix of lower price supports and deficiency payments was continued in the 1973 farm legislation. Events of the 1970s led policymakers (and agricultural producers) to believe they had created perfection. The export boom of the 1970s raised world market prices to the point where the support prices were inoperative, deficiency payments unneeded, and production controls irrelevant. Agricultural export earnings rose every year from 1969 through 1981; they reached a peak of $44 billion with 162 million tons of commodities. Farm program costs were low during those years of rising nominal prices and export volume.

Since the rising nominal world market prices made it cost-free, each successive renewal of farm legislation (in 1977 and 1981) mandated higher support prices and higher target prices. In addition, support prices for grains were raised in 1980 to offset the market effects of the embargo on grain exports to the Soviet Union, which was imposed in response to the Russian invasion of Afghanistan. The US dollar began to strengthen appreciably in 1981 and, by mid-1985, was up some 40 percent against other major currencies. As world trade slackened and world market prices slumped, US support prices became the umbrella for world agricultural commodity prices.

In 1982 the US government began to acquire large quantities of commodities under its price support programs, and US agricultural exports began to fall. For instance, world wheat trade fell from 101.3 million tons in 1981/82 to 84.9 million tons in 1985/86. Over this same period, US wheat exports fell from 48.2 million tons to 25.0 million tons as others expanded output and exports. World trade in coarse grains fell from 107.8 million tons in 1980/ 81 to 83.3 million tons in 1985/86. US exports fell from 70.7 million tons to 36.4 million tons in the same years. Similar sharp declines were registered in cotton and rice exports. At the same time, with grain prices falling and dairy price supports rising, dairy production rose rapidly. With dairy product prices supported, surplus stocks of manufactured dairy products skyrocketed, resulting in huge government costs for acquisition and storage.

In 1983, in an act of desperation, the US government resorted to a massive land-retirement program, which was paid for through surplus commodities owned by the Commodity Credit Corporation (CCC), the government price-stabilization agency. It was the payment-in-kind (PIK) program. In total, 77.9 million acres of land were withheld from crop production in 1983. The harvested acreage of wheat was reduced by 16.5 million acres, and that of corn by 21.2 million acres. In addition, corn and soybean yields were reduced sharply by drought, and domestic and international grain prices rose in response to the artificial shortage. The reaction was short lived, however, and prices resumed their downward trend by mid-1984 when surplus commodity stocks began to rise again.

In late 1985 the basic farm legislation governing US grains, oilseeds, and sugar was rewritten. The Reagan administration proposed lowering price supports by tying them to an average of market prices during a recent period. The target prices and deficiency payments were to be phased out completely over a five-year period. It was believed that, as a result, expenditures on farm price and income supports would be sharply reduced over time.

US agriculture, however, was squeezed by the worst collapse in farm-asset values in a half century. Declining farm prices, falling asset values, and record real interest rates created a widespread financial crisis among debt-leveraged farmers. This led to widespread farm bankruptcies and the closing of numerous farm banks and rural farm community businesses.

In the face of this financial distress, the US Congress was not willing to adopt a program that would sharply reduce government support for the agricultural sector. The program it passed had three objectives: to maintain farm income, to expand US agricultural exports, and to contain or reduce federal budget expenditures on farm price and income supports. Congress chose to freeze the target prices of major crops for two years and then reduce them modestly and gradually in an attempt to maintain producers' income.

The expansion of US agricultural exports was to be accomplished by dual action: the basic price supports were sharply lowered and, in the case of cotton and rice, effectively removed; and export subsidies were mandated in the form of direct export subsidies, increased subsidized credit, and a new 10-year export-credit program.

Budget controls were to be achieved by requiring acreage reductions as a condition for receiving government deficiency payments and by freezing the base yields upon which deficiency payments are calculated.

US farm prices, export prices, and world prices for major commodities fell beginning in late 1985, and the declines continued through 1986 as lower US support prices, export subsidies, large world supplies, and slow economic growth all pushed in the same direction. The gap between US target prices and world prices has widened appreciably as world prices have declined.

In July 1986 congressional pressure to broaden export subsidies to all commodities and all destinations caused the administration to agree to subsidize wheat exports to the Soviet Union. This was not enough to satisfy congressional critics who added additional export subsidies to 1987 trade legislation.

Australia and Argentina bitterly protested the US export subsidies on wheat and their extension to more markets. The Australians threatened to reconsider their defense-base arrangements with the United States, and the Argentines threatened to halt payments on their foreign debt in retaliation. Thailand strongly protested the new US rice program that pays US producers large deficiency payments and allows US exporters to sell at any price. Competing cotton export producers have protested the US cotton program, which initially dropped world cotton prices to about 25 cents per pound, 40 cents below a year earlier.

Perhaps the most significant reaction came from Canada, which ruled, in response to a petition from Canadian corn growers, that the US target-price payments and certain other programs constitute a countervailable subsidy on corn and related products entering Canada. The US government has taken the issue to GATT charging that the Canadian action is not legal under the GATT subsidy code because the Canadian industry cannot prove injury. If the GATT rules against the United States, other countries might also take action on other commodities.

Budget costs of US farm programs have followed a different path from those of the EC (table 4.2). US costs fell sharply in the mid-1970s and remained relatively low until 1982, at which point surplus accumulation and falling export prices began to escalate program costs. The federal budget expenditures for farm prices and income support rose sixfold between 1982 and 1986. It was estimated that fiscal 1986 program costs were in excess of $25 billion, 50 percent above the previous high and three-fourths as high as total net farm income. A single cotton producer is reported to have received payments of $20 million, while 400 rice producers shared deficiency payments of some $400 million.

The 1985 farm bill also contained a provision for long-term retirement of marginal land under a government payment system. Under this program farmers sign contracts taking land out of production for 10 years in return for government payments. As a result of this, together with the land set-asides required to gain eligibility for price support programs, total acreage idled in the United States will be about 70 million in 1987. The massive subsidies, acreage reductions, and price changes have brought an end to the economic deterioration in US agriculture. In 1987, land prices appear stabilized and both exports and farm income are increasing.

Several US agricultural commodities have had sharply different policies from those of the export-oriented commodities. These include sugar, dairy products, tobacco, and peanuts.

Increasingly tight production controls on tobacco and peanuts have been used to reduce domestic output and to maintain high internal prices. The internal price of peanuts for edible use is protected by zero import quotas under the Section 22 exemption accorded to the United States in the GATT. Domestic tobacco producers have tried twice since 1980 to get the US government to invoke the same type of import quotas for tobacco and have both times failed to win the approval of the US International Trade Commission (USITC). As a result, the domestic support price for tobacco had to be lowered drastically in 1986 to avoid increased imports and to regain export competitiveness.

The major feature of the tobacco and peanut programs is the value that has arisen related to rights to produce the crop. Holders of these historical rights have enjoyed an economic rent that has been bid into the prices of the land to which the quotas are attached.

Governmental action on behalf of sugar and intervention in sugar trade goes back further than for any other agricultural commodity in the United States. The first US tariff on raw sugar was imposed in 1789. For nearly 200 years, the United States has maintained import duties on all imported sugar, except for raw sugar imported from 1890 to 1894.

In 1934 a program for sugar was developed that lasted 40 years—a program of production and import quotas that allocated domestic consumption between domestic and foreign growers. Domestic growers were subject to acreage

TABLE 4.2   **Net US budget expenditure for farm price and income support[a]**
(million dollars)

Commodity	1970	1971	1972	1973	1974	1975	1976	1977
Feed grains	1,439.5	1,069.3	1,722.1	1,215.9	552.6	200.3	124.3	659.2
Corn[b]	1,096.7	847.7	1,422.1	1.025.7	444.2	150.1	111.8	400.4
Barley	79.2	24.1	21.3	74.6	45.7	12.6	7.1	77.8
Oats	103.7	74.5	55.6	−59.1	−86.7	−20.8	−15.7	42.3
Sorghum	152,9	114.5	215.6	166.4	144.1	58.7	21.5	139.0
Wheat and	795.5	467.6	866.9	73.0	241.6	21.7	68.5	1,899.3
wheat products	765.8	430.7	831.0	359.1	208.6	25.5	70.2	1,898.9
Rice	38.6	41.6	5.4	21.6	14.7	c	166.6	144.6
Soybeans	−160.7	−606.5	−64.9	−20.7	26.4	−21.9	−9.2	4.8
Vegetable oil products	−15.8	20.3	20.8	18.6	16.3	−0.8	0.1	−0.5
Upland cotton	891.4	603.2	760.4	824.0	724.6	232.8	8.2	104.3
Sugar	—	—	—	—	—	—	—	—
Dairy	87.1	217.4	174.2	116.6	46.0	424.4	40.1	469.1
Support/rel.	3,776.8	2,821.8	3,983.4	3,555.3	1,004.1	574.9	1,014.4	3,809.2
Net CCC/PL480	4,776.7	3,818.7	5,065.9	4,383.3	1,744.8	1,519.2	1,804.8	4,669.8

Source: History of Budgetary Expenditures, Fiscal Years 1961–1979, 28 December 1979 (Book I) and *Fiscal Years 1980–1986*, 29 December 1986 (Book II), Commodity Credit Corporation, Budget Division, ASCS, USDA.

restrictions, minimum wage laws, and child labor provisions. Import quotas were assigned to foreign countries.

This system was abandoned when the law was not renewed in 1974 during a period of soaring sugar prices. However, falling world sugar prices caused the US Congress to include a provision in the farm legislation of 1977 requiring a minimum support level for sugar. World prices fell enough so that the CCC accumulated surplus sugar in 1977 and 1978 that was subsequently resold at a profit as world market prices rose.

The 1981 and 1985 farm legislation again required a minimum support price for sugar. As world market prices fell, import quotas were invoked on

1978	1979	1980	1981	1982	1983	1984	1985	1986ᵃ
2,288.3	1,143.8	1,286.0	−532.6	5,397.1	6,814.5	−758.4	5,210.8	12,211.5
1,697.0	866.5	1,256.3	−666.5	4,280.6	5,719.6	−933.7	4,402.7	10,523.8
178.8	96.5	−26.6	49.6	128.6	267.8	89.2	335.9	471.0
25.0	−10.6	−12.7	−20.2	−1.5	11.2	4.4	1.5	26.2
388.0	190.4	67.8	103.9	988.5	813.7	75.5	463.4	185.0
844.3	308.4	878.6	1,542.6	2,237.5	3,418.9	2,536.1	4,690.8	3,439.7
840.3	300.2	866.0	1,536.5	2,230.0	3,410.0	2,522.1	4,645.6	3,390.5
−66.1	49.5	−75.8	24.0	163.5	664.4	332.9	989.6	947.0
31.1	3.5	116.0	86.7	169.2	287.7	−585.0	711.3	1,597.4
5.2	12.2	10.9	7.9	23.6	−1.5	13.0	12.2	17.9
223.8	141.2	64.3	335.7	1,189.7	1,362.9	244.0	1,552.7	2,141.9
394.7	312.6	−405.2	−120.6	−5.5	49.0	10.2	184.8	213.6
240.1	23.8	1,011.1	1,893.8	2,182.2	2,528.1	1,502.5	2,084.7	2,337.0
5,623.4	3,572.1	2,717.2	3,994.2	11,598.3	18,757.3	7,183.5	17,573.8	25,718.5
6,464.6	4,587.4	3,825.1	5,290.1	12,581.6	19,842.9	8,400.9	19,398.3	26,936.5

a. Minus sign indicates that total receipts exceeded total outlays. Fiscal years 1 July to 1 June to 1977 (1976–77 transition year). The 1986 figures are preliminary.
b. The 1981 and 1984 figures show major receipts from repayments on commodity loans and from sales receipts for payment-in-kind.
c. Less than $50,000.

sugar under Section 22 to prevent government accumulation of surplus sugar stocks. Despite these quotas, a sugar surplus was accumulated and was sold to China at a fraction of its cost in August 1986. This sale was strongly protested by Australia as unfair trade.

The effect of the program has not been to expand the domestic output of sugar. Instead, the program has provided a profitable umbrella for the expansion of sugar substitutes for sweetener use. In 1978 the total per capita consumption of all caloric sweeteners was 126.6 pounds. Refined sugar made up 72 percent of this consumption. By 1985, consumption of all caloric sweeteners had risen to 129.8 pounds, but sugar had fallen to 48.8 percent of the total. Even though the use of sweeteners had risen, the total consumption of refined sugar fell from 10.18 million to 7.58 million short tons in eight years. Since domestic sugar production was more or less stable, all of the decline in sugar consumption fell on imports, which were reduced accordingly. If recent trends continue, domestic sweetener production will fill domestic requirements completely and, by 1990, all imports will be ended. The United States, like the EC, could become a sugar exporter.

The price support program for dairy products has operated through purchases of manufactured dairy products—butter, cheese, and nonfat dry milk—by the CCC. Import quotas are used to limit the imports of manufactured dairy products and to maintain domestic prices above world prices.

Dairy output grew at record rates in the early 1980s, as a result of rising productivity, which more than offset declining cow numbers. As a result, the CCC had to remove nearly 17 billion pounds of milk equivalent from the market in 1983. This led Congress to authorize the first program to pay farmers to leave the dairy business. By 1985, milk production had resumed its rapid upward trend, spurred by lower feed prices. In the 1986 farm bill, Congress mandated a whole-herd buy-out program. This program paid farmers to terminate dairy production and stay out of it for five years. It mandated that the cows in the exiting herds either be slaughtered or exported. It further mandated that 200 million pounds of beef be exported to offset the effects of the program on domestic beef prices. This beef was purchased by the government and sold abroad at a fraction of the acquisition price.

The US Department of Agriculture (USDA) announced that the buy-out program would reduce milk production by 12.3 billion pounds over 18 months at a cost of $1.8 billion. The average cost of the program was estimated to be $14.88 per hundred weight of milk removed from production. The average domestic price for milk at the time was $12.40 per hundred weight.

Because of the high cost of accumulating and holding stocks of surplus dairy products, the United States has become an increasing exporter of dairy products at subsidized prices.

The US domestic policy, like EC policy, turned out to be based on incorrect assumptions regarding world market conditions. World market conditions in the 1980s do not permit both high target prices to protect farm income and low program costs. Moreover, with stagnant world markets, even sharply lower domestic prices and extensive export subsidies are not large enough to increase exports sufficiently to prevent continued surplus accumulation.

The expanded use of export subsidies, and the payment of deficiency payments on all production tied to target prices well above world prices, have brought increasing criticism from foreign competitors. The United States has claimed that it has resorted to export subsidies only to compete with other export subsidies.

The US program, like the EC program, is under increasing pressure at home because of budget costs, not because of its adverse trade effects. As of mid-1987, the political pressures are toward increasing rather than decreasing export subsidies, despite mounting protests from abroad.

Other OECD Countries

Other OECD countries' agricultural policies generally follow the EC model. West European countries generally maintain high internal prices via import controls and use export subsidies to dispose of surpluses.

Canada and Australia have followed different directions. For their major export crops they use marketing boards, which are given sales monopolies, and which sell at competitive prices in world markets. Canadian exports are aided by subsidized rail rates to export points. Canada also has a stabilization fund financed by producers and government, which pays producers if aggregate income falls below certain previous levels. Canada uses import controls and production controls under marketing boards to maintain producer prices for dairy products, poultry, meat, and some horticultural products at above world prices. Australia protects domestic producers of certain products via import controls or tariffs.

New Zealand, which is heavily dependent upon agricultural exports, makes extensive use of marketing boards in exporting agricultural products, but has few or no direct government export subsidies.

Until recently, Canada and Australia took pride in the fact that they had little or no direct government subsidization of their grain growers. In late 1986, however, the Canadian government announced that about 1 billion Canadian dollars would be paid to improve growers' incomes. And early in 1987, the Australian government found it would be required to make payments to the Australian Wheat Board to make up the shortfall in funds needed to cover advance payments to growers, which could not be met from export sales.

Developing Countries

Whereas most developed countries use policies that maintain prices and/or returns to agricultural producers at well above world market prices, most developing countries maintain internal prices, both to producers and consumers, at levels below world market levels. This is accomplished by the use of state monopolies or marketing boards for imports and exports, state controls over internal marketing, and export taxes.

The net effect of these policies tends to be that internal farm prices are depressed below world prices, consumers in urban areas are subsidized, and import dependence is increased. In a few cases, internal producer prices are kept high by state purchases, and subsidized resale to consumers allows lower consumer prices.

One notable exception to this generalization is Korea, which has followed a different route, one closer to policies followed by Japan than to other developing countries. Korea maintains an extensive array of import controls and state trading to keep most internal agricultural prices well above world prices. As in the case of other countries with similar policies, domestic production now exceeds demand at these high prices and surpluses of some products have appeared.

In some cases, differential export taxes are applied on raw products to increase the export of processed products. Brazil and Argentina have used such a tax on soybeans to increase processors' margins and to maintain low internal prices. Malaysia uses a differential export tax on palm oil to ensure the export of processed oil.

For most developing countries, the political appeal of low prices to urban consumers has outweighed the interests of agricultural producers. In some cases, there has been an attempt to offset the depressing effects of the controls and taxes by heavily subsidizing agricultural credit, fertilizer, and other agricultural inputs. In most cases, this web of governmental interventions has reduced agricultural output by reducing producers' incentives.

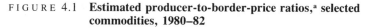

FIGURE 4.1   **Estimated producer-to-border-price ratios,ª selected commodities, 1980–82**

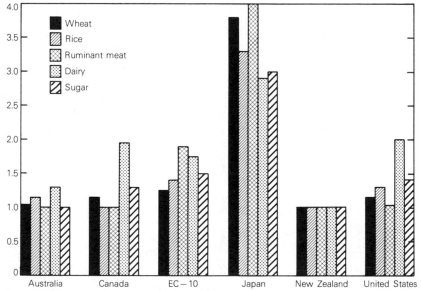

Source: Rodney Tyers and Kym Anderson, "Distortions in World Food Markets: A Quantitative Assessment" (a background paper for *World Development Report 1986*, World Bank, Washington). a. Domestic producer prices divided by border prices. The weighted averages are calculated using 1980–82 production at border prices for weights.

Levels of Protection Provided by the Programs

There are great differences in the way in which the agricultural programs of different countries operate. Overall, however, they provide different levels of protection for producers in various countries. In recent years, various attempts have been made to measure these levels of protection.[2]

Two recent attempts have received wide attention. One is the studies by the OECD, which measure the producer subsidy equivalent (PSE) of the various programs. Another has been developed by Tyers and Anderson: figures 4.1 and 4.2 show the levels of protection for major commodities and

2. A review of these measures and others, and of some trade models, is found in *Agricultural Trade Model Comparison: A Look at Agricultural Markets in the Year 2000 With and Without Trade Liberalization*, Rachel Nuget Sorko, Discussion Paper Series No. RR87–01, Resources for the Future, November 1986.

FIGURE 4.2   **Estimated producer-to-border-price ratios,[a] selected commodities, 1980–82**

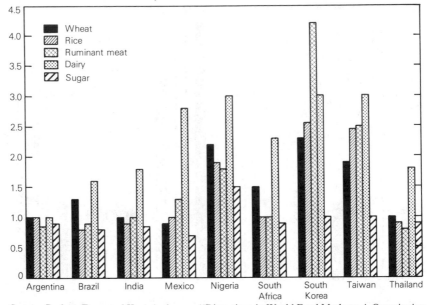

Source: Rodney Tyers and Kym Anderson, "Distortions in World Food Markets: A Quantitative Assessment" (a background paper for *World Development Report 1986*, World Bank, Washington).
a. Domestic producer prices divided by border prices. The weighted averages are calculated using 1980–82 production at border prices for weights.

countries as computed by Tyers and Anderson for 1980–82. The USDA has extended the OECD studies and updated them to 1982–84. One of the summary tables from their work is shown as table 4.3. Despite the difference in methods and time periods, the results point in the same direction. In terms of levels of protection by countries, Japan is the highest, followed by South Korea, Taiwan, Nigeria, and the European Community.

In terms of commodities, the highest levels of protection around the world are for dairy producers and for producers of beef and veal. There are, of course, major variations from country to country and from one commodity to another, but, in general, the differences are greater between countries than within a single country. The notable exception is dairy producers, who receive substantial protection even in countries where average levels of protection are low.

Ranking of producer subsidy equivalent levels, commodities by country, 1982–84

Ratio[a]	United States	Australia	Canada	New Zealand	EC-10	Japan
Producer tax						
−.25 to −.49						Citus
Producer subsidy						
0 to .09	Beef Pork Poultry meat* Soybeans*	Barley* Beef* Cotton* Pork* Poultry meat* Sheep meat* Wheat* Wool*	Beef Corn Oats* Pork* Soybeans	Barley* Wheat	Corn	
.10 to .24	Barley*	Cane sugar* Manufactured milk Rice*	Barley* Flaxseed* Poultry meat Rapeseed* Rye* Wheat*	Beef* Fluid milk Manufactured milk* Wool*	Barley* Common wheat* Pork*	
.25 to .49	Corn* Cotton* Dairy* Rice* Sorghum* Wheat*	Fluid milk	Sugar	Sheep meat*	Dairy* Durum wheat* Poultry meat* Rapeseed Rice Sheep meat Soybeans Sugar*	Poultry meat
.50 to .74	Sugar		Dairy*		Beef*	Beef Pork Soybeans Sugar
.75 to .99						Barley Fluid milk Manufactured milk Rice Wheat

TABLE 4.3 *continued*

Ratio	Taiwan[b]	South Korea[b]	India	Argentina	Nigeria	Mexico	Brazil
Producer tax							
More tax than −.50					Cocoa* Sugar		
−.25 to −.49			Cotton (LS)* Wheat	Wheat*			
−.10 to −.24			Cotton (MS)* Peanut meal Rice	Corn* Sorghum* Soybeans*			
−.01 to −.09			Rapeseed meal Soybeans Soymeal		Rice Cotton		Soybeans* Corn Beef*
Producer subsidy							
0 to .09	Pork*				Corn		Manufactured milk Poultry meat*
.10 to .24	Corn Soybeans Sugar*	Poultry meat	Peanuts* Rapeseed			Cotton*	
.25 to .49	Beef Dairy Poultry meat Rice* Tobacco	Pork	Peanut oil Rape oil Soy oil		Wheat	Sorghum Soybeans Wheat	Cotton* Rice
.50 to .74	Sorghum Wheat	Barley Beef Corn Fluid milk Rice Soybeans Wheat				Corn	Wheat
.75 to .99							

Source: Government Intervention in Agriculture, Economic Research Service, USDA, Staff Report No. 229, April 1987.
* = Net exporter during 1982–84
a. Ratio of policy transfers to gross domestic value of production including direct payments.
b. Impacts of input subsidies not included.

Protection and Trade Distortions

Levels of protection do not automatically translate into trade distortions. To measure accurately the trade distortions resulting from the present programs, a general equilibrium model is needed to predict what the world would look like if the various programs were removed. Such a model needs the supply elasticity and cross-elasticities and the price and income elasticities for all major commodities in all countries.

Several of these models exist, as well as some partial equilibrium models that look at individual commodities. One of the most comprehensive and well-known is by Tyers and Anderson, which provided the background material for the *World Development Report 1986*.[3] While the individual models give somewhat different results, depending upon the specific model and its supply and demand coefficients, they dictate the general direction of shifts that would occur if the government interventions were removed.

Some estimates from the Tyers and Anderson study illustrate both the effects of the programs and why they will be difficult to remove. Table 4.4 shows estimates of the price and trade effects of total trade liberalization on major products. It suggests that, except for ruminant meat and dairy products, world prices would rise only modestly if liberalization occurred in industrial market economies. Trade volume would rise appreciably in coarse grains, rice, ruminant meat, dairy products, and nonruminant meat. However, as the table shows, it is the policy changes in the EC and Japan that would account for the major portion of the changes in trade volume. The model implies a reasonably high supply elasticity in both cases, and a high price elasticity of demand in Japan in response to lower prices.

Table 4.5 also shows the same aggregate data as affected by the total liberalization of markets in developing countries. Except for rice (down) and dairy products (up), world prices would not be much affected. However, trade volumes of rice, meats, dairy products, and sugar are estimated to increase significantly. In other words, supply sources would shift drastically but total supply and demand would not.

If both developing countries and industrial market economies liberalized trade, the model shows that trade volume would increase appreciably in all commodities but wheat. Prices in world markets would rise for all commodities

---

3. Rodney Tyers and Kym Anderson, "Distortions in World Food Markets."

TABLE 4.4   **International prices and trade effects of total liberalization of GLS markets in developing and industrial market economies, 1985[a]**

	Wheat	Coarse grain	Rice	Ruminant meat	Non-ruminant meat	Dairy products	Sugar
International price level (percentage change)							
IMEs	2.0	1.0	5.2	16.1	1.5	27.0	4.9
Developing countries	6.8	3.4	−12.4	−0.1	−3.6	35.9	3.2
Total IMEs and developing countries	8.8	4.2	−7.9	15.9	−2.1	66.9	7.6
World trade volume							
Developing countries							
Ton change (thousand)	7,440	11,550	8,160	1,940	6,710	92,250	14,800
Percentage change	7	12	75	68	260	330	60
IMEs							
Ton change (thousand)	−900	18,140	3,450	5,560	460	26,160	390
Percentage change	−1	19	32	195	18	9	2
Total IMEs and developing countries							
Ton change (thousand)	6,400	28,900	10,650	6,720	7,660	51,990	14,880
Percentage change	6	30	97	235	295	190	60

IME   industrial market economy. GLS   Grains, livestock products, and sugar markets.
Source: Rodney Tyers and Kym Anderson, "Distortions in World Food Markets: A Quantitative Assessment," table 24.
a. Excluding Cuba.

but rice, but the rise in most would be small—the exception being dairy products. Surprisingly, it shows that the policies of developing countries depress the trade volume in sugar, dairy products, rice, and nonruminant meat more than the policies of the industrial market economies! If one looks only at the industrial market economies, the major market impact of their policies is to distort the market for meat and dairy products.

TABLE 4.5   **Effects on economic welfare of total liberalization of GLS markets in industrial market economies, 1985[a]**
(billion 1980 dollars per year)

	Producer welfare	Consumer welfare	Total welfare	Foreign exchange earnings	Total welfare (dollars per capita)
Industrial market economies	−55.6	101.9	48.5	−38.6	64.0
Australia	0.6	−0.2	0.3	0.7	20.0
Canada	−1.8	1.0	0.2	−1.1	10.0
EC-10	−22.7	42.6	22.3	−21.8	82.0
EFTA-5	−5.0	7.5	3.6	−2.5	115.0
Japan	−11.7	39.6	23.5	−14.5	196.0
New Zealand	0.5	−0.2	0.3	0.6	87.0
Spain and Portugal	−0.9	3.1	1.5	−1.0	32.0
United States	−14.6	8.5	−3.2	1.0	−14.0
Centrally planned Europe	26.8	−24.1	−11.1	7.5	−26.0
USSR	18.4	−17.7	−9.2	5.2	−34.0
Other Eastern Europe	8.4	−6.4	−1.9	2.3	−14.0
Developing economies	27.8	−29.9	−11.8	21.3	−3.0
Egypt	0.5	−0.7	−0.6	0.3	−14.0
Nigeria	0.3	−0.6	−0.5	0.3	−5.0
South Africa	0.7	−0.6	−0.3	0.6	−8.0
Other sub-Saharan Africa	1.7	−1.9	−0.6	2.0	−2.0
Other North Africa and Middle East	2.4	−4.1	−1.8	0.5	−9.0
Bangladesh	0.5	−0.4	0.0	0.5	0.0
China	4.2	−3.8	−2.0	3.1	−2.0
India	5.8	−5.8	−2.2	3.7	−3.0
Indonesia	0.7	−0.7	−0.3	0.6	−2.0
Korea	0.6	−0.8	−0.5	0.1	−12.0
Pakistan	1.8	−1.5	−0.5	1.5	−5.0
Philippines	0.2	−0.3	−0.1	0.2	−1.0
Taiwan	0.2	−0.2	−0.1	0.1	−4.0
Thailand	0.3	−0.3	0.1	0.4	2.0
Other Asia	1.0	−1.2	−0.4	0.4	−2.0
Argentina	1.2	−1.0	0.3	1.8	12.0
Brazil	1.7	−1.9	−0.6	2.0	−4.0
Cuba	0.3	−0.3	0.0	0.5	−1.0
Mexico	1.8	−1.7	−1.2	0.9	−16.0
Other Latin America	1.9	−2.1	−0.5	1.8	−4.0

GLS Grains, livestock products, and sugar markets.
Source: Tyers and Anderson, table 21.
a. Includes change in government revenue.

Another set of the Tyers and Anderson calculations shows why trade negotiations to remove domestic programs will be difficult. Tables 4.5, 4.6, and 4.7 show the producer and consumer welfare changes and the foreign exchange effects of liberalization. If the industrial market economies (IMEs) liberalized, producer welfare in those economies would be reduced by $55.6 billion: producers in developing countries would gain $27.8 billion, and in Eastern Europe and the USSR about the same amount; producers' losses would be very large in the EC, Japan, the United States, and the European Free Trade Association (EFTA). The foreign exchange earnings of the IMEs would fall by $38.6 billion, with the United States, New Zealand, and Australia showing slight gains. The developing countries would gain $21.3 billion, the biggest gainers being India, China, Brazil, Argentina, and Pakistan.

The biggest gainers from liberalization of IMEs would be their own consumers, whose welfare would increase by $101.1 billion. This would accrue mostly to consumers in the EC and Japan. The big consumer losers would be in Eastern Europe, the USSR, and almost all developing countries. The total welfare in developing countries would decline because consumers would pay a higher price than they are now paying for both domestic supplies and imports.

If only the developing countries liberalized, almost the reverse would occur. Producers' welfare in IMEs would increase, that of producers in developing countries would decrease. The balance of payments gains would accrue to IMEs. The EC would be the biggest gainer in both producer income and foreign exchange, the United States second.

If both IMEs and developing countries liberalize (but not Eastern Europe and the USSR), a different result emerges. The aggregate producers in both groups lose, with the largest losses in the EC, Japan, the United States, EFTA, and Korea. Consumers in both blocs gain, at the expense of consumers in Eastern Europe and the USSR. Foreign exchange of both IMEs and importing developing countries worsens, and Eastern Europe benefits.

Total liberalization has a positive effect upon producers' welfare in Australia, New Zealand, Argentina, Brazil, Thailand, and some other Latin American and Asian developing countries. This, of course, explains the support of these countries for total liberalization. However, total producer welfare is reduced in all other IMEs and most developing countries. Consumer welfare increases sharply in both developed and developing countries outside Eastern Europe and the USSR.

TABLE 4.6   **Welfare effects of total liberalization of GLS markets in all developing economies, 1985**

(billion 1980 dollars per year)

	Producer welfare	Consumer welfare	Total welfare[a]	Foreign exchange earnings	Total welfare (dollars per capita)
Industrial market economies	33.9	−27.5	−10.2	16.3	13.0
Australia	0.6	−0.5	0.0	0.4	3.0
Canada	1.5	−1.0	−0.2	1.0	−8.0
EC-10	17.5	−13.9	−4.3	9.0	−16.0
EFTA-5	3.5	−2.6	−1.0	1.2	−33.0
Japan	−0.6	0.7	−0.4	−0.3	−4.0
New Zealand	0.4	−0.2	0.2	0.5	52.0
Spain and Portugal	0.9	−1.1	−0.8	0.4	−16.0
United States	10.1	−8.9	−3.7	4.1	−16.0
Centrally planned Europe	29.8	−25.0	−13.1	7.1	−31.0
USSR	21.1	−18.9	−10.7	5.6	−39.0
Other Eastern Europe	8.7	−6.1	−2.4	1.5	−18.0
Developing economies	−22.5	56.6	28.2	−28.6	8.0
Egypt	−0.5	1.4	0.9	−1.0	19.0
Nigeria	−2.3	5.2	1.7	−3.2	17.0
South Africa	−0.6	0.9	0.3	−0.8	9.0
Other sub-Saharan Africa	−0.1	1.9	1.5	−0.4	5.0
Other North Africa and Middle East	−4.8	8.8	0.6	−3.1	3.0
Bangladesh	−0.6	0.1	−0.5	−0.6	−5.0
China	−4.6	13.9	10.9	−7.3	11.0
India	−2.1	2.5	1.5	−2.3	2.0
Indonesia	−2.6	5.7	3.5	−4.3	22.0
Korea	−5.2	11.8	5.1	−4.0	126.0
Pakistan	−0.4	1.0	0.4	−1.4	4.0
Philippines	−0.3	0.8	0.0	−0.2	0.0
Taiwan	−1.3	2.3	1.1	−1.0	58.0
Thailand	0.4	−0.3	−0.2	0.7	−3.0
Other Asia	1.6	−1.3	0.2	−0.7	1.0
Argentina	1.6	−1.2	0.1	2.0	2.0
Brazil	0.9	−0.9	−0.7	1.4	−6.0
Cuba	0.3	−0.3	−0.1	0.4	−7.0
Mexico	−2.8	4.8	2.2	−3.7	29.0
Other Latin America	0.9	−0.5	−0.3	0.9	−2.0

GLS   Grains, livestock products, and sugar markets.
Source: Tyers and Anderson, table 30.
a. Includes change in government revenue.

TABLE 4.7 **Effects on economic welfare of total liberalization of GLS markets in industrial market and developing economies, 1985[a]**
(billion 1980 dollars per year)

	Producer welfare	Consumer welfare	Total welfare	Foreign exchange earnings	Total welfare (dollars per capita)
Industrial market economies	−39.2	83.2	45.9	−26.1	60.0
Australia	1.0	−0.5	0.4	1.1	25.0
Canada	−1.1	0.4	0.3	−0.3	12.0
EC-10	−13.1	32.9	22.1	−14.7	81.0
EFTA-5	−3.7	6.2	3.6	−1.9	114.0
Japan	−12.0	39.3	22.9	−14.5	192.0
New Zealand	1.0	−0.4	0.5	1.2	161.0
Spain and Portugal	−0.5	2.3	1.1	−0.9	23.0
United States	−10.8	3.0	−5.0	3.9	−21.0
Centrally planned Europe	61.7	−49.3	−23.1	17.1	−55.0
USSR	43.3	−36.8	−19.1	12.7	−70.0
Other Eastern Europe	18.4	−12.5	−4.0	4.4	−29.0
Developing economies	−2.8	26.9	18.3	−6.1	5.0
Egypt	−0.4	0.7	0.3	−0.8	6.0
Nigeria	−2.1	4.6	1.2	−2.9	12.0
South Africa	−0.2	0.4	0.2	−0.2	5.0
Other sub-Saharan Africa	1.4	0.3	1.2	1.6	4.0
Other North Africa and Middle East	−3.3	5.9	−0.9	−2.9	−4.0
Bangladesh	−0.2	−0.3	−0.5	−0.2	−5.0
China	−1.6	7.4	7.4	−2.5	7.0
India	2.0	−2.8	0.3	1.6	0.0
Indonesia	−2.1	4.8	3.1	−3.9	19.0
Korea	−5.0	11.2	4.7	−4.1	115.0
Pakistan	0.8	−0.4	0.1	0.1	1.0
Philippines	−0.1	0.6	0.0	−0.1	−1.0
Taiwan	−1.1	2.1	1.1	−1.0	55.0
Thailand	0.7	−0.5	−0.1	1.2	−2.0
Other Asia	2.5	−2.6	−0.2	−0.2	−1.0
Argentina	3.1	−2.3	0.5	4.1	17.0
Brazil	1.5	−2.6	−1.0	3.5	−8.0
Cuba	0.6	−0.5	−0.1	0.9	−7.0
Mexico	−2.0	3.3	1.5	−3.1	20.0
Other Latin America	2.7	−2.4	−0.5	2.8	−3.0

GLS Grains, livestock products, and sugar markets.
Source: Tyers and Anderson, table 34.
a. Excluding Cuba.

Of course, there would be major changes among different producer groups within many countries. In the United States, for instance, dairy and sugar producers would lose, while feed grain and meat producers would gain.

The measurement of levels of protection and trade distortions were made in the early 1980s. The relative levels of protection have increased significantly in many countries since that period.[4] Because world market prices have declined, while internal prices have not, trade distortions have increased. This implies that world prices for most commodities would increase more from 1987 levels than is implied by the modest changes shown in the models. Indeed, Tyers and Anderson now estimate real international agricultural price increases averaging 31 percent in 1995. This average included a 3 percent increase for coarse grains to a 95 percent increase for dairy products.[5] This, in turn, would increase possible consumer-welfare gains and producer losses in some cases. Most important, it would provide for bigger gains for the low-cost producers.

One can argue the specifics of the changes the model estimates, but in general the direction of change appears sensible and consistent with the observed levels of protection. These estimates indicate why it will be politically difficult to negotiate away the current levels of protection afforded by agricultural programs. Most developed countries have already proven the extreme difficulty of reducing these agricultural subsidies unilaterally to achieve either budget savings or consumer benefits. The prospects of doing so in a multilateral forum do not appear much better, even though the adjustments involved would be less. In most trade negotiations, consumer interests are not the overwhelming issue that drives national negotiations.

---

4. An updated run of the Tyers and Anderson model indicated protection ratios in 1988 in OECD countries will be 50 percent above 1980–82 levels. See Rodney Tyers and Kym Anderson, *Liberalizing OECD Agricultural Policies in the Uruguay Round: Effects On Trade and Welfare,* Working Papers in Trade and Development no. 87/10, Australian National University, July 1987.

5. Ibid. p. 23 and table 3.

5 The Rules for Agricultural Trade in the GATT

Changes in the General Agreement on Tariffs and Trade (GATT) rules relating to agriculture are crucial, if not the major issue for many countries entering the new round of multilateral trade negotiations. The euphemism generally applied to GATT objectives is to "make GATT rules apply to agriculture." The fact, however, is that the GATT rules *do* apply to agriculture. But the rules in certain areas relating to agriculture are inconsistent with the way the GATT deals with nonagricultural industries.

To understand the controversy over the GATT rules relating to agriculture, it is necessary to briefly review the early history of the formation of GATT and the important place that the United States had in its founding.

Special treatment of agriculture surfaced immediately when the US delegation to the preparatory conference for the International Trade Organization, which led to the present GATT, recognized that the US Senate would not ratify an international agreement that would have forced the United States to dismantle its agricultural program or which would have made its programs inoperable.[1] Thus the United States, which was one of the major participants in the founding of the GATT, insisted on special rules for agriculture, even though such treatment was opposed strongly by a number of other countries.

The differences between the approach to agriculture and the approach to other industries in the GATT are fundamental. In general, GATT rules relate to how governments may intervene to protect domestic markets and industries. They also spell out how countries relate to each other in terms of rights and obligations under trade rules. These general rules were agreed to by member countries of GATT, and governments brought their practices in line with these rules.

---

1. For a history of the development of GATT and the effect of US agricultural policy on it, see William Adams Brown, Jr., *The United States and the Restoration of World Trade* (Washington: The Brookings Institution, 1950).

For agriculture, the process was exactly the reverse. The GATT rules were written to fit the agricultural programs then in existence, especially in the United States. Since then the rules have been adopted or interpreted to fit various other national agricultural policies. So instead of developing domestic agricultural policies to fit the rules of international trade, we have tried to develop rules to fit the policies. Not surprisingly, this has not worked very well.

Opposition to special treatment for agriculture came from two sources. On one hand, certain countries, such as Australia, whose agricultural policies did not require the use of export subsidies, vigorously opposed special treatment for agriculture. On the other hand, a number of the important developing countries, which were largely agricultural and had a substantial interest in developing domestic manufacturing, were opposed to special treatment for agriculture unless they, too, could have similar rules to protect and develop their domestic manufacturing industries.

US Policy and GATT Rules in Agriculture

It is useful to recall the agricultural policy context in a number of countries at the time in which the GATT rules were written. As mentioned earlier, the United States had passed its basic agricultural legislation in the Agricultural Adjustment Act of 1933. The objective of the legislation was to stabilize the prices of the farm commodities that had been suffering from the worldwide economic collapse of the 1930s. The basic legislation, an intervention mechanism for agriculture, included production control programs, internal commodity price supports at above world levels, and the authority for the Commodity Credit Corporation (CCC) to use export subsidies to maintain or increase the exports of US farm products. It also contained the authority for the President to impose tariffs and quotas if imports of commodities from foreign sources threatened the workability of the domestic price support programs in the United States.

The European Community did not exist in the late 1940s when the GATT was founded. The Treaty of Rome was not signed until 1957, and the common agricultural policy (CAP) did not emerge in its full-blown form until the early 1960s. At the time that the GATT was conceived, Japan was struggling to recover from wartime devastation and scrambling to feed its population. A number of the important developing countries were still colonies or were newly emerging independent nations which had not yet had the opportunity to develop and put into place the agricultural policies that they were to follow in the 1960s, 1970s, and 1980s.

Not only did agriculture receive special treatment in the GATT, but the special treatment also appears to have been tailored to the US farm programs then in existence. The special treatment revolved around two issues: subsidies and quantitative restrictions. It is ironic that three decades later these special exceptions for agriculture would become the major focus of the US government's efforts to change the rules in the current GATT negotiations.

Subsidies in the GATT

It is generally recognized that the GATT rules relating to trade treat agriculture differently from every other industry. This is more evident on the subsidy issue than for any other issue. As will be discussed later, this separate treatment has been the source of most of the agricultural trade disputes that have been taken to the GATT.

The subsidy provisions of the GATT have a tortuous background. The Havana Charter for the stillborn International Trade Organization had subsidy language, but the original GATT articles had only a section that required any contracting party to report "any subsidy, including any form of income or price support, which operates directly or indirectly to increase exports of any product from, or to reduce imports of any product into its territory, to other parties." In other words, the original GATT articles contained no prohibition on subsidies, domestic or export.[2] That form became what is now Article XVI:1. Later, the prohibition against export subsidies on other than primary products was added as Article XVI:4.

In 1955, Article XVI was extended. Article XVI:2 recognized that export subsidies may have harmful effects. It is followed by the now famous Article XVI:3, which says, "Accordingly, contracting parties should seek to avoid the use of subsidies on the export of primary products. If, however, a contracting party grants directly or indirectly any form of subsidy which operates to increase the export of any primary product from its territory, such subsidy shall not be applied in a manner which results in that contracting party having more than an equitable share of world trade in that product, account being taken of the shares of the contracting parties in such trade in

---

2. Members adversely affected by subsidies also could ask for consultations to discuss the possibility of limiting subsidization. It has not proven an effective control.

the product during a previous representative period, and any special factors which may have affected or be affecting such trade in the products.''

When Article XVI:4 (which prohibits export subsidies for other [nonprimary] products) was made a part of the GATT, the separate treatment of agriculture was complete. It specifically prohibits export subsidies on all products other than primary products.

Subsequent attempts have been made to clarify and extend the Article XVI:3 provisions relating to trade in primary products. The most recent attempt was made in the context of the negotiation of the GATT Subsidies Code during the Tokyo Round, completed in 1979. These efforts concentrated on trying to further define ''equitable market share'' and ''representative period.'' Severe price undercutting via subsidies also was ruled off limits. As it turns out, however, this attempt did not solve any significant problems and most of them are still unresolved.

Experience Under the Subsidies Code

Disputes over subsidies and quotas have dominated the area of agricultural trade. A total of 14 subsidy disputes were taken to the GATT between 1948 and 1985. Eight of these occurred in the last decade, and all eight were subsidy disputes in agriculture. Moreover, it is over these subsidy cases that the dispute-settlement process in the GATT has broken down, yet another indication of fundamental differences between countries concerning special treatment of subsidies for agriculture.

All of the subsidy cases taken to the GATT have involved one or more European countries, now members of the EC. These disputes date back to 1957 and have sharply increased in frequency since 1975, about the time when the EC became a major force in world markets via the use of export subsidies.

The subsidy cases include eggs (one in 1957), flour (two in 1958 and 1981), barley (one in 1977), sugar (two, in 1958 and 1982), and pasta (one in 1982). Complaints against the EC have been filed by Australia, Brazil, Chile, and the United States.[3]

Most of the controversy over the special rules relating to subsidies in

---

3. For a summary of GATT cases, see US International Trade Commission, ''Review of the Effectiveness of Trade Dispute Settlement Under GATT and the Tokyo Round Agreements,'' Report to the US Congress, Senate, Committee on Finance, December 1985.

agriculture has centered on the inability of the disputants and the panels that have heard the cases to determine what constitutes an equitable share of the world market. Until this concept of equitable market share is resolved, the subsidies code as it now pertains to agricultural export subsidies is likely to continue to be a bone of contention. Indeed, many countries, including the United States, have concluded that this part of the GATT articles must be changed drastically.

Two agricultural subsidy cases are notable in other respects. In 1982 the United States charged that EC export subsidies on pasta were illegal because pasta is not a primary product covered by the special rules. The GATT panel that heard the case ruled in favor of the US position, agreeing that pasta was not a primary product and that, therefore, subsidies on it were not covered by the special exemption for primary products.

In another case, the United States charged that EC domestic production subsidies on canned fruit, which were paid to processors, nullified or impaired tariff concessions granted by the EC on imported fruit. The subsequent panel report agreed with the US position. This case is interesting in that it is one of the few cases when a GATT panel has explicitly acknowledged that domestic subsidy programs do disrupt trade. The panel's landmark decision establishes an argument against those who view export subsidies as the only source of trade distortion.

In retrospect, it appears that two important assumptions underlie the GATT rules in agriculture. One is that many countries would intervene in agricultural markets using measures that would maintain their internal prices above world prices. And, it has turned out, this has been true. The second assumption is that the nations should be able to compete in the export market through the use of export subsidies, as long as these exports do not displace others in the world market.

The present subsidy rules imply a market-share approach to world agricultural trade. This, of course, has substantial implications for all countries involved in the agricultural trade situation; for a number of countries, this implication is clearly not an acceptable one under current conditions.

The significance of this issue for some countries was highlighted by a meeting in Cairns, Australia, in late August 1986 of 14 agricultural exporting countries that pledged to fight in the new Uruguay Round for the complete abolition of agricultural subsidies that affect trade over a period of time.[4]

---

4. The countries are Argentina, Australia, Brazil, Canada, Chile, Colombia, Fiji, Hungary, Indonesia, Malaysia, Philippines, New Zealand, Thailand, and Uruguay.

They demanded that the GATT place agriculture under the same rules that have been applied to nonagricultural commodities. If implemented, this change would involve phasing out all export subsidies on agricultural products and eliminating all domestic subsidies affecting agricultural trade.

Quantitative Restrictions

The GATT rules relating to quantitative restrictions in trade constitute another area where the treatment of agriculture in GATT is different from that of other products.

Four GATT articles deal with quantitative restrictions: Article XI prohibits the use of quotas (with certain exceptions), Article XII provides for an exception to Article XI for balance of payments reasons, Article XIII outlines the rules to be followed in cases where quotas are applied on imports or exports, and Article XIV provides exceptions to Article XIII under certain balance of payments situations. As far as agriculture is concerned, it is the exceptions under Article XI and the rules in Article XIII that are of interest.

As in the case of subsidies, the differential treatment of agriculture related to quantitative restrictions also was controversial from the beginning. Developing countries objected to agricultural exceptions, imposed by developed countries, that allowed quantitative restrictions on products for which developing countries were low-cost producers. Developing countries also objected to rules that prohibited them from using quantitative restrictions to protect their infant-manufacturing industries from foreign competition.

The agricultural exceptions in Article XI:2 are:

● Export restrictions can be used to prevent or relieve critical shortages of foodstuffs or other products essential to the exporting country.

● Import and export restrictions can be used to bring about "the application of standards or regulations for the classification, grading, or marketing of commodities in international trade."

● Import restrictions may be applied on any agricultural or fishery product imported in any form necessary to the enforcement of governmental measures that operate to: restrict the production or marketing of the like domestic product or of a domestic product that is a close substitute; remove a temporary surplus of a like domestic product by making the surplus available to groups of domestic consumers free or at reduced prices; or restrict the quantities produced of any animal product that is directly dependent wholly or mainly on the imported commodity.

In practice, as was the case of the article on export subsidies, the programs were written to fit the US agricultural programs that were in place at the time. Anyone familiar with US agricultural programs will recognize that one set of provisions is to protect crops that have domestic marketing orders or agreements operating under the US system. Another is to allow import controls on products that have domestic price support and production-control programs. Article XI:2 (c)(iii), which allows restrictions of products used in animal production, is not clear. The United States has never had serious production control programs for any animal products, but it appears that this section might have possibly been added in the event that production controls were applied to animal products.

Even after writing these special rules allowing for quantitative restrictions on agricultural imports, largely to fit the US programs, the United States soon found it could not live with what it had agreed to. In 1951 the Congress said, "No trade agreement could be applied in a manner inconsistent with this section (section 22 of the Agricultural Adjustment Act)." In 1955 the United States insisted upon and received the famous "temporary" waiver, under the threat that it might otherwise be forced to leave the GATT. The waiver is still in effect more than 30 years later and is used to restrict imports of sugar, peanuts, and dairy products.

The United States was thus given the right under the GATT to put quantitative restrictions on imports of agricultural commodities that materially interfere with the operation of any of its domestic agricultural programs. Whereas under Article XI other countries are supposed to take actions that restrict the production or marketing of the domestic product, this waiver allows the United States to apply import restrictions without regard to such rules. In practice, the waiver is of major importance only for sugar and manufactured dairy products, where quantitative import quotas have been in place without domestic production control programs for long periods of time.

This waiver, which provides different sets of rules for the United States than for other countries, has been a source of continuing resentment by other countries and is regularly used by others to argue that the United States is not serious about trade liberalization in agriculture.

Complaints under Article XI in the field of agriculture have been relatively limited, perhaps because the GATT rules and practices on quantitative restrictions (QRs) in agriculture are so loose. In 1986 the United States asked a GATT panel to determine whether Japanese QRs on 12 agricultural products, originally imposed for balance of payments reasons under Article XII, are now consistent with GATT obligations. Moreover, as will be discussed later, the use of state-trading agencies as a method of controlling all imports and exports of agricultural commodities provides a convenient way to restrict imports or control exports without imposing QRs under Articles XI and XIII.

Since it was recognized that import quotas were likely in agriculture, Article XIII set up rules for applying them. It basically applies the most-favored-nation approach to quotas. Article XIII:1 states that if quotas applied, they must apply to all imports from all sources or to all exports to all sources. Article XIII:2 states that if quotas are used, they shall aim at a distribution of trade approaching as closely as possible shares that could be obtained in the absence of quotas. Article XI:2(c) also includes a provision that says restrictions ''shall not be such as will reduce the total of imports relative to the total of domestic production, as compared with the proportion which might reasonably be expected to rule between the two in the absence of restrictions.''

However, the purpose of QRs usually is to alter the proportion of imports relative to domestic production. Therefore, these rules regarding the avoidance of trade distortion implied in the GATT rules generally are not followed. Very few disputes on this issue, however, are brought to the GATT.

Another provision states that when quotas are allocated to countries, a representative period should be used to determine the allocation. This provision is intended to take abnormal crop years and trade patterns into account and avoid discrimination in the application of trade restrictions.

If a serious attempt at trade liberalization is to occur in the current round of GATT negotiations, the issues that must be addressed include the rules relating to the use of quantitative import restrictions and whether these rules are relevant in the present world. In recent years, the United States has tried to get other countries, especially Japan and Korea, to remove their import quotas on agricultural products. Thus far the removal of these quotas has proved difficult. One of the reasons often cited is the continued use by the United States of import quotas for dairy products and sugar under conditions that would clearly be outside the GATT rules were it not for the Section 22 waiver granted to the United States.

In the current GATT negotiations, there will be great resistance to allowing the United States or any nation to retain special exemptions from the rules applying to all other nations. Realistically, no country now has the dominant economic and political position enjoyed by the United States at the time of the GATT's founding.

A number of countries have insisted that unless the United States is willing to put its Section 22 waiver on the bargaining table, the prospect for substantial liberalization of agricultural trade is quite dim.

State Trading in Agriculture

GATT rules relating to state trading have always been difficult in concept and even more so in their application. Conceptually, the GATT views a world of private firms operating in a competitive environment. Government interventions in such a world come in the form of tariffs, quotas, and subsidies.

The world of agricultural trade is quite different. Government intervention in agriculture comes in many forms, but the use of state monopolies, or state-authorized monopolies, is pervasive. Whereas state trading might have been viewed largely as an instrument of socialist governments, in agricultural affairs such entities also are widespread in "market" economies. In some cases only imports and exports are involved; in other cases internal trade also is reserved for state monopolies.

It is estimated that as much as 90 percent of world trade in wheat passes through such governmental agencies, and about 70 percent of trade in coarse grains. Countries using such agencies range from China and India to Japan, Canada, and Australia.

GATT rules relating to state trading basically have two elements:

● that state-trading entities operate on a nondiscriminatory basis, governed only by commercial considerations

● that entities with import monopolies negotiate a limit on the level of protection applied in the form of a price mark-up.

In reality, neither of these provisions has been enforced, so that states that use such entities have essentially been free to operate without regard to rules normally applied to trade.

For instance, a country using state trading in a product can limit imports, and thus maintain high internal prices without resorting to overt import quotas. Japan does this with wheat and uses the profits from the sales of wheat to millers to finance part of its expensive rice program. The Japanese policy prohibiting rice imports and restricting beef imports also operates under this GATT section.

On the export side, state agencies can be used to sell products abroad at prices well below domestic prices without resorting to export subsidies (as the term is normally defined). Canada and Australia both make use of this practice through their Wheat Boards, which sell at high statutory prices internally and export without benefit of government payments at much lower prices.

There is no indication that any major attempt will be made in the present GATT round to reform the rules relating to state trading in agriculture. If this is the case, most of the trade liberalization being discussed for agricultural trade will not apply to most developing countries or to many products both imported and exported by developed countries.

Other Import Controls

Two widely used forms of import protection are not formally covered by GATT rules. One is the voluntary restraint agreement (VRA), and the other is the variable levy.

Voluntary restraint agreements probably are not as pervasive in agriculture as they are in the manufacturing sector, but they have been widely used as a method of controlling imports. At present the EC has such an agreement with Thailand to limit tapioca imports, to plug the potential gaps left by the tariff bindings on nongrain feed substitutes. The United States has used them periodically to avoid invoking its Meat Import Act, legislation that would probably be found contrary to GATT rules if tested under Article XI as there are no price support programs or production controls for meat.

Voluntary restraint agreements, of course, are not voluntary. They are put in place because the exporting country fears or is threatened with import controls that would be less favorable. VRAs have the full impact of quotas without the importing country's having to adopt the conditions required in Article XI.[5]

5. C. Fred Bergsten, Kimberly Ann Elliott, Jeffrey J. Schott, and Wendy E. Takacs, *Auction Quotas and United States Trade Policy*, POLICY ANALYSES IN INTERNATIONAL ECONOMICS 19 (Washington: Institute for International Economics, 1987).

The variable levy is another instrument used to control imports that falls outside the tariffs envisioned by the GATT founders. As an import device it is ingenious, since it offers absolute protection against all outside producers, regardless of their efficiency. It also offers complete isolation from world market forces to producers behind its protection. Technically, its status under GATT rules has never been determined.

Given the various devices that have been developed outside of the GATT rules to control imports and protect domestic programs in agriculture, it is no wonder so few cases regarding import controls have gone to GATT.

Movement Toward Change

These problems and deficiencies in GATT rules relating to agriculture have been a rising source of dissatisfaction for some time. After a stormy ministerial meeting in 1982, a special committee on agriculture was formed to examine these rules. The committee gathered a wide spectrum of opinion about the direction new rules might take.

At about the same time, the Organization for Economic Cooperation and Development (OECD) launched a series of studies on the kinds and extent of protection afforded the agricultural sector in member countries. A series of country studies was completed using a common method (called producer subsidy equivalents, or PSEs) to measure agricultural protection. In May 1987 the OECD Ministers approved a statement suggesting that these levels of protection be scaled back and that farm income protection be carried out in ways that reduce the adverse effects upon trade. The heads of state of the largest industrial nations also endorsed this approach in Venice in June of 1987.

Thus, after almost four decades of experience with GATT rules written and interpreted to fit national agricultural programs, there appears to be a growing consensus that an attempt should be made to adjust domestic agricultural programs to fit a common set of rules regarding trade in agricultural products. This, as will be seen, is the thrust of the agricultural negotiations in the Uruguay Round and, as such, marks a major departure from previous negotiations.

6 Framing the Issues

Once trade negotiations are seriously under way, they take on a life of their own as nations usually play out whatever political lines they were pursuing early in the negotiations. At the end, there are often agreements for the sake of agreement, and the goals originally being pursued are lost in the euphoria of a new accord. Therefore, it is important to have a checklist of issues that need to be dealt with in the context of the agricultural negotiations.

One basic issue overrides all the other issues that must be faced in this trade round. That issue is whether agriculture at both the national and international levels will be a managed industry or an industry where competitive forces are allowed to operate. This is not a case of crying "Wolf." The present condition in world agricultural trade is not politically stable. Currently, new subsidies and new import-protection devices are being added regularly to counter programs of other countries. Under this system, countries with vast treasuries will certainly defeat countries with sparse treasuries. Even so, in one way or another, all countries are losers in the present situation. It is the realization that unilateral reform is difficult and risky and the present direction disastrous that pushes them toward fundamental reform in a multilateral framework.

As is usually the case, no clear-cut decision or rapid shift from one direction to another will be made. At best, the general outcome of this negotiation will be a shift in direction. The direction that is set will likely be followed for a long time.

Several issues will arise in the negotiations. One argument is that the agricultural industry is unique and requires special rules to meet its special characteristics. This position appeals more to agriculturalists than to mining, forestry, and manufacturing interests that face similar supply and demand conditions and many of the same adjustment problems.

Nevertheless, the virtues of treating agriculture exactly the same in GATT as other industries are also overstated. In most economies, agriculture is not treated the same as other domestic industries, and most of the trade difficulties

115

flow from that simple fact. After forty years of separate treatment in the GATT, the problem is not whether the same rules apply to agriculture as to other industries, but whether *any* agreed-upon set of rules can be developed that allows agricultural resources to be used fully, efficiently, and in a way that lets countries benefit from, instead of fight over, agricultural trade.

Another diversionary issue will be whether the negotiations should justifiably supersede national social policy that in many countries has concluded that farmers, landowners, or other selected parties (rural voters) are to receive special income transfers. This is not a real issue, for the answer is obviously no. A successful trade negotiation cannot attempt to negotiate domestic welfare policies. There can, however, be trade negotiations that agree to limit the policy mechanisms used to bring about income transfers to instruments that least distort resource use and world trade flows.

Setting the Framework

The GATT member nations have embarked upon a unique round of trade negotiations in agriculture. For the first time they have agreed to trade negotiations that deal directly with their domestic agricultural policies and the adverse trade effects of those policies. This much is understood and agreed. However, much of the negotiations will actually be over exactly what was meant by the general agreement contained in the Punta del Este Declaration.

This unique trade negotiation is beginning in an unusual period in world agriculture. The slowdown in world demand growth and excess capacity in agriculture has led to severely depressed international prices for many traded items. These problems have been exacerbated by a rising level of protection and subsidies that have further depressed and disorganized world markets.

Trade negotiations normally do not concern themselves with near-term market conditions. Currently, however, these market conditions are so depressed and so much dependent upon government policies that they cannot be ignored. Thus, it appears necessary to broaden the scope of these negotiations to include dealing with the immediate short-run situation.

This means the negotiations must deal with three related issues: 1) market stabilization; 2) freezing present subsidy programs; and 3) negotiating new rules regarding subsidies and import barriers in agricultural trade.

THE ELEMENTS OF MARKET STABILIZATION

Some persons, mainly in the United States, will argue that attempts to deal with market stabilization 1) are unlikely to succeed, and 2) will remove the pressure now felt by many countries to negotiate changes in their agricultural policies. The fact that these two arguments are inconsistent does not appear to bother those advancing them.

The arguments for some coordinated efforts that would help stabilize markets are those of necessity. There is a demonstrable excess capacity in world agriculture, much of it induced by government programs. Measures are needed to offset these output-increasing subsidies until the subsidies themselves can be altered.

No one has argued that these programs can or should be ended abruptly. In the past few years these various agricultural programs also have led to an excessive stock accumulation of grains, dairy products, beef and veal, and some other widely traded products. The governments that hold these stocks have a great desire to reduce them. Thus, these stocks represent a continuing threat to market stability and affect the willingness of countries to undertake needed policy changes.

A market-stabilization program should include three elements:

• production restraints or efforts to offset the current incentives to maintain excess resources in agriculture

• an agreement on guidelines for the disposal of surplus stocks held or controlled by governments

• a freeze on *all* access barriers and subsidy programs in agriculture.

The latter would lead directly and logically into the heart of the negotiations, i.e., how to improve access and reduce the adverse impact of subsidies on trade.

RESTRAINING EXCESS CAPACITY

Substantial excess capacity in world agricultural production relative to current world markets, if allowed to continue to feed into world markets or swell surplus stocks, could further worsen the already difficult trade and commodity price situation. Therefore, a temporary ad hoc arrangement on capacity reduction needs to be developed as an adjunct to the trade negotiations. Measures taken by countries to adjust capacity should not be counted either for or against the participating country in terms of the trade negotiations.

The purpose of the program should be made clear and agreed upon from the outset. It would not be to fix global agricultural output. It would not be to try to create artificial scarcities that would push agricultural commodity prices above the long-term equilibrium levels. And it would not be to fix world market shares at levels many countries would consider unfair. The capacity-adjustment program should have the simple objective of removing some of the excess measures induced into production by government programs. It would relieve the continued downward pressure on world agricultural prices, which are now well below any conceivable equilibrium price, and keep countries from dumping products resulting from current excess capacity and excess stocks into international markets. Together with the freeze on subsidies, it would allow countries that try to reduce their agricultural capacity to do so without having other countries take advantage of the situation.

Several simple principles should be applied in considering such adjustments. First, no nation should take steps to reduce excess capacity in one commodity (for example, grains or sugar) by pushing its productive resources into the production of other commodities.

Second, if excess capacity is dealt with by stock building, these stocks subsequently should be managed so that they do not displace potential trade, internally or externally.

Third, since government assistance (subsidies) would almost certainly be required to remove excess capacity, such assistance should be organized and paid in a way that does not further increase production incentives or reduce consumption.

Finally, countries will have differing abilities to contribute to such capacity adjustment, depending on their economic circumstances. Moreover, countries have had varying levels of the government intervention that has helped create excess capacity. Those with high levels have the major responsibility for taking measures to deal with the problem. However, the mere fact that countries have or have not engaged in domestic or export subsidies should not be the only criterion for participation, nor should a country's status as a net importer or net exporter.

The problems of developing countries that have operated without heavy subsidies in agriculture need special attention. While the stabilization of the world market would significantly benefit many of them, in many cases they lack the funds to compensate producers for internal production adjustment. However, such countries could, at minimum, avoid actions that would stimulate output or encourage exports at the expense of participating countries.

Specific methods of achieving the desired and agreed-upon adjustments will have to be left to national policies. For instance, in the United States, land retirement is the preferred policy to adjust production, and over 70 million acres were idled under 1987 farm programs. The European Community (EC) has proven that production quotas with heavy penalties for excess output can limit or reduce dairy output induced by high supported prices. Canada has used delivery quotas on wheat successfully in the past. Sugar and sweetener production are relatively easy to control, if desired, because the raw materials pass through processing plants.

At the beginning it should be recognized and agreed that the production-adjustment program would be temporary and subject to annual review. Several countries have carried out such programs unilaterally for their own political and economic reasons, usually because of budget considerations. They should receive credit for such programs (where due) and continue them. However, to use coordinated production adjustment as a permanent or long-term approach to trade is, in fact, explicit market sharing, which, in the long run, is trade restrictive, not trade increasing.

REDUCING EXCESSIVE STOCKS

One of the most obvious manifestations of the agricultural subsidy problem is the accumulation of excess stocks by an agency of the government that attempts to maintain domestic farm prices in excess of market-clearing levels.

The stock buildup has several adverse effects. First, storage costs for all agricultural commodities are high, and they are especially high for such perishables as butter, nonfat dry milk, and meat. Thus, stock buildups result in very large costs that are charged as agricultural subsidies when, in fact, the money goes to nonfarm storers of the surpluses. Second, the presence of these stocks, and the constant likelihood they will be moved into world markets at fire-sale prices, depresses prices of the stockpiled products.

There is no good measure of appropriate stock levels of various commodities. For dairy and meat products, which are continuously produced throughout the world, stocks are not needed outside pipeline stocks, carried in commercial trade channels. In the 1970s there was a great effort to develop a grain-stock policy to avoid sudden surges in the price of grains due to crop shortfalls. Even then, the actual level of the stocks needed was found to be relatively small compared with total world output.

The current excess stocks are large in several commodities. The United States will enter the 1987/88 wheat marketing year with a carry-over of 52 million tons of wheat, which is twice the current annual export level and equal to 92 percent of the previous year's production. The United States will enter the 1987/88 coarse grain marketing year with 174 million tons of coarse grain stocks, nearly five times the previous year's exports and more than total domestic use. The EC has 17 million tons of surplus grains, and the governments of India, Pakistan, and Saudi Arabia all have higher grain stocks than they desire. The EC has 1.5 million tons of surplus butter, a million tons of dried milk, and three-quarters of a million tons of beef in storage. In total, stocks of wheat and coarse grains outside the United States have risen 55 million tons since 1982/83.

These stocks are largely under governmental control around the world and, therefore, freezing subsidies to producers does not automatically deal with them. This means that there must be some kind of general understanding regarding the disposal of these excess stocks.

That understanding should be achieved by all countries that have stocks in excess of their desired level and should address three issues: the current level of stocks, by commodity, held or controlled by the government; the desired level of stocks of these same products; and plans for the disposal of the stocks, including the time over which the disposal would occur. It is not possible to outline a detailed stocks-disposal program in this study. However, given the context in which it will occur, some obvious rules would seem relevant.

The first rule is that stocks disposal should not be a source of increased exports to further depress world prices and displace other exports. Second, domestic disposal should aim at disposal through increased consumption unless domestic production controls are used to reduce production by an offsetting amount. Third, disposal in domestic markets should avoid the direct displacement of imports.

The stocks-disposal program cannot proceed without a freeze on subsidies, and the freeze is unlikely to be meaningful unless there is a parallel stocks-disposal understanding. Present production levels are continuing to build stocks in a number of countries and will do so even with a freeze on current subsidy levels.

Thus, what is needed is a total and comprehensive approach that involves extraordinary measures to deal with an extraordinary situation, one that will get worse before it gets better in the absence of such action. Normally, major trade negotiations can begin immediately with the specific trade matters to be negotiated. This is not the case for agricultural issues at this time. Anything short of a comprehensive approach will make the actual negotiations on trade-related policies impossible.

CHANGING THE RULES

The heart of the multilateral trade negotiations (MTN) in agriculture should consist of a three-part exercise:

- freezing subsidies and import barriers

- agreeing on the terms of reference as to which agricultural programs should be brought under GATT discipline

- deciding how to bring the various programs under international rules.

A freeze on agricultural subsidies and import barriers is a logical starting point in the negotiations for several reasons. One compelling reason is that if this negotiation is to succeed it must show at an early stage that the countries participating in the negotiations are serious about the issues they are facing. This has led the United States to push for an "early harvest" or "fast track" for agriculture, which has been strongly resisted by other countries.

It is hypocritical at best for countries to agree, as they did at Punta del Este in September 1986 and at the OECD in Paris in May of 1987, that subsidies ought to be reduced or changed, and then proceed to increase the very trade-distorting measures they have set out to remove. Yet, this is exactly what has happened during 1987. The US Congress is pushing to expand US export subsidies, the EC proposed a new tax on fats and oils, and the Canadians have increased subsidies to their producers.

The concept of a freeze thus has become a test of the credibility of the process that has been put in motion. There has been talk of an "early harvest" in this MTN round; yet if it is not possible politically to even call a halt in the steady escalation of subsidies, it appears unlikely that negotiating a retreat can be achieved.

The US government has been among those opposing such a freeze. The argument has been that if the pressure of increasing subsidies is removed, the willingness to negotiate changes will also disappear.

This is not a plausible argument, especially if a freeze is tied to an agreed-upon timetable for the remaining parts of the agricultural negotiation. If progress is not made in the negotiations it is always possible for a country to further increase subsidies if it believed that such actions would increase the likelihood of a successful negotiation.

An unwillingness to have a cease-fire while negotiating rules for peace implies that some of the parties are seeking an unconditional surrender. That, however, is not how trade wars end.

Dealing with Subsidies and Import Barriers

The first decision that must be addressed is what the objectives of the negotiations really are regarding these domestic programs and it is already clear that different countries have different views regarding the objectives in the ministerial declaration launching the Uruguay Round.

First, the contracting parties agreed "there is an urgent need to bring more discipline and predictability to world agricultural trade by correcting and preventing restrictions and distortions including those related to structural surpluses so as to reduce the uncertainty, imbalances and instability in world agricultural trade." However, this statement by itself could be interpreted to mean almost anything, including that world agriculture should be organized into commodity agreements and arrangements similar to present textile trade under the Multi-Fiber Agreement.

The declaration goes on to say:

Negotiations shall aim to achieve greater liberalisation of trade in agriculture and bring all measures affecting import access and export competition under strength-ened and more operationally effective GATT rules and disciplines, taking into account the general principles governing the negotiations, by:
(i) improving market access through, inter alia, the reduction of import barriers;
(ii) improving the competitive environment by increasing discipline on the use of all direct and indirect subsidies and other measures affecting directly or indirectly agriculture trade, including the phased reduction of their causes;
(iii) minimizing the adverse effects that sanitary and phytosanitary regulations and barriers can have on trade in agriculture, taking into account the relevant interna-tional agreements.

In reference to existing GATT articles the declaration states: "Participants shall review existing GATT articles, provisions and disciplines as requested by interested Contracting Parties, and, as appropriate, undertake negotiations."

These statements indicated that, for the first time since the inception of the GATT, member countries feel they must rewrite the GATT rules relating to agriculture in ways that put agreed limits on subsidies and import barriers arising from domestic agricultural programs. The direct links between current domestic agricultural programs, structural surpluses, and trade distortions finally appear to have been officially recognized. This recognition alone marks a great step forward in dealing with the problems.

What is omitted from the declaration is also telling. No reference is made to the uniqueness of agriculture or its special adjustment problems or to food security or the special role of food trade. These points, which have been used so often in so many countries to justify government programs that prevent adjustment, will not disappear as political forces in the negotiations; but the fact that they are not included in this basically political document is of some significance.

The analysis that follows has the basic assumption that nations agreeing to the negotiation have, in fact, the following objectives:

● to reduce import barriers of all types for agricultural products

● to provide agreed disciplines for the use of all present and future direct and indirect subsidies

● to phase out the negative effects of any existing subsidies.

These objectives do not mention the elimination of import barriers or the phasing out of all subsidies. Even so, these negotiations are the most comprehensive international attempt ever undertaken to deal with the web of governmental interventions, a web that has developed from the hitherto lack of any international disciplines over the multitude of national agricultural policies.

These negotiations will be drastically different from most other trade negotiations either in agriculture or in other products. In general, GATT negotiations have focused on tariffs, subsidies, dumping, and certain codes of conduct. But when venturing into the never-never land of agricultural policies, new issues and new ground must be broken if progress is to be made.

Understanding this difficult task, it is necessary to look briefly at the major domestic and border measures now in use that need to be dealt with if the negotiation is to achieve its objectives.

IMPORT CONTROLS

In this area the basic and most difficult assignment will be to determine the measures to be included in the negotiations. The following is an extensive, but not exhaustive, list of trade-distorting measures that should be covered in the negotiations.

Tariffs.   In general, tariffs are not the major element in agricultural import controls, but where they exist they should, of course, be included. Special attention should be given to the differential tariffs between raw and processed products that protect domestic food-processing industries.

Quantitative restrictions.   These abound in agricultural trade, most operating outside the bounds of Article XI of GATT.

Mixing regulations.   A number of countries impose a series of mixing regulations upon food processors and manufacturers that effectively serve as QRs on imports.

Health and sanitary regulations.   Almost every country imposes health, sanitary, and/or labeling regulations on agricultural products and foodstuffs. Many of them are disguised trade restrictions and have little or no relationship to health and sanitary needs.

Variable levies.   Despite widespread agreement that the variable levies of the EC member states and other countries are among the most disruptive protective devices employed in agricultural trade, their status under GATT rules is not clear.

Minimum import prices.   This is another device that does not currently fall under GATT rules but which may have a substantial impact on trade.

Voluntary restraint agreements.   These devices also do not fall under GATT disciplines, yet they have become a major way of imposing de facto import restrictions with the same effect as import quotas.

State trading.   State trading is the most common way of controlling imports of agricultural products. In theory, this matter is covered under GATT Article XVII, but in practice nothing happens. If a negotiation on reducing import barriers occurs without addressing the state-trading issue, it cannot be considered a serious negotiation. Moreover, with China formally applying to join the GATT and the Soviet Union expressing interest, this may be the last chance to deal with the issue.

SUBSIDIES

The ministerial declaration regarding subsidies was a unique departure from past trade negotiations in that all participating nations agreed to discuss "the use of all direct and indirect subsidies and other measures affecting directly or indirectly agricultural trade." Given the large number of such subsidies imbedded in the agricultural systems around the world, this promises to be a difficult, if not impossible, task. Therefore, it is important that, as a first step, the negotiators develop a strategy.

Nowhere does the declaration say that the use of subsidies should be discontinued, only that discipline should be increased when using subsidies and that "their negative effects" should undergo a "phased reduction." A curious phrase follows the preceding statement that apparently was added at US insistence and after much negotiation. This phrase, "and dealing with their causes," with all respect to its drafters, seems irrelevant to the issues. If it refers to subsidies, their causes are political; and if it refers to negative effects, their causes are the subsidies.

The negative effects of subsidies are obvious. They encourage production of goods that would not otherwise be produced or they alter consumption patterns in the countries affected or both. There is a danger that the causes will be overdefined, as is often done by economists. It is largely irrelevant that the subsidies generally reduce consumer welfare or that they drain public coffers. These are of value for discussions of welfare economics but not for trade negotiations. Welfare issues and public-expenditure issues are a proper subject for domestic politics, but bringing them into the trade discussions would overload the system.

There is also a danger of defining low world commodity prices as one of the effects of the subsidies. If this is done, there will be a push to look at export-market sharing, commodity agreements, and other devices for international price fixing as feasible methods of reducing the negative effects of subsidies.

If, and it is a big if, an agreement could be reached that a simple definition of what constitutes a negative effect will suffice, then the more important issue of what forms of subsidies have undesirable effects and how those effects can be limited may be addressed.

The United States has proposed that OECD measures of levels of effective protection (PSEs) be considered the measure of trade-distorting effects of subsidy programs. This concept, however, measures the income transfers of the subsidies, not the supply, demand, and trade effects. For instance, the US target price and deficiency-payment program based upon output clearly provides a significant level of income subsidy to commodity producers. It also provides an incentive to produce, subject to whatever constraints in the form of production controls are in place. However, deficiency payments do not reduce consumption of the products concerned, in either the domestic market or the world market. Indeed, the general complaint against the US programs under the 1985 Food Security Act is that the deficiency payments depress world prices by encouraging output without providing market support.

For operational and negotiating purposes, a subsidy should be defined as "any program operating through government, or using powers granted by governments, that results in producer prices (including payments) that are above prices in world markets for the products involved."

A reason for using a broad and simple definition of subsidies is to avoid the trap in which programs that do not involve the expenditure of government funds are considered not to involve a subsidy. Such a claim is made for the EC sugar program, which fixes a very high internal price, pushes sugar into world markets at world prices, and defrays export losses by a producer-financed levy on the higher priced domestic sales. Such programs have a siren appeal to public officials under pressure to reduce public expenditures, for they can under certain conditions reduce public expenditures to zero. When this practice is used by private businesses, it is called dumping and considered illegal under GATT rules (if it causes injury); there is no reason to assume it is less harmful when condoned and/or carried out by governments.

The conditions under which such programs will work are relatively easy to define. First, the domestic demand for the product must be relatively inelastic, implying it has no close substitutes in use. Second, the domestic market demand at the high price must be a large fraction of total output so that relatively small increases in domestic prices produce enough revenue to cover losses on exports. Third, it must be possible to control and measure output receiving the high price. Finally, the product must be one where it is possible to extract revenue from consumers without a political reaction.

Of course, such a scheme will not work for exporters whose domestic population and consumption are small relative to the production of the commodity. Thus, countries like Argentina and Australia would be at a severe disadvantage if such programs were considered not to be subsidies (since their populations are so small relative to their production of products like wheat, oilseeds, and beef).

The EC is moving toward the same program in grains, even though the necessary conditions do not exist. The demand for grains for feed is much more elastic because some animals can use forage as well as grains. Most important, however, is the ability to substitute nongrains, such as soybeans, tapioca, and corn gluten feed, which enter levy free. Finally, whereas sugar and beets all pass through a central processing plant, grains for feed do not and, since many are used on the farms where they are produced, interfarm sales are common. Thus, unless individual farm quotas are established, no real control can be established over output, and no penalty or tax can be charged to pay for export losses.

CLASSIFYING SUBSIDY EQUIVALENT MEASURES

Once "subsidy" has been defined, the various measures in use can be classified relatively easily according to whether or not they fall under the definition. If they do, they should be dealt with in the negotiation on rules.

The real focus of the negotiations comes down to the issue of rule making regarding the future. There are three possibilities for each type of subsidy: allow them without limit, limit them, or agree to ban them.

In all likelihood, the number of existing subsidy programs that countries will agree should have no restrictions will be fairly large. Certainly, there is no pressure or strong argument to limit subsidies such as public agricultural research, product utilization research, or public infrastructure investment. There already are international rules regarding concessionary export sales that are now classified as food aid. Changes in those rules on concessionary sales, if needed, could be more appropriately dealt with in context of the Food Aid Convention, which includes recipients as well as donor countries.

The greatest difficulty will be to find agreement on which subsidies should be banned entirely as unfair trade practices. A number of countries will push vigorously for the complete banning of export subsidies. Other countries or groups, especially the EC, will insist that a ban on export subsidies is incompatible with their domestic agricultural policies and would destroy them. In such cases, it would be desirable to consider a two-pronged approach: first is to ban certain subsidies for products where they do not now exist; second is to limit the use of such subsidies where they do exist.

The most difficult negotiations and greatest dangers fall in the in-between area of trying to achieve rules to limit subsidies, or to "limit their impact upon trade." It should be noted that the current GATT rules for subsidies in agriculture used this approach and it has failed completely. Article XVI limits subsidies to those that do not produce more than an equitable market share and says they should avoid substantial price undercutting. In markets as volatile as agricultural commodity markets, in which significant shifts in export availability and import requirements occur, no amount of refinement is likely to make the present concepts workable short of overt, precise, and continuous market sharing.

By focusing only on trade effects when attempting to negotiate subsidies, this problem is most likely to arise. Ultimately, three effects are at issue— the output effect, the consumption effect, and, thus, the trade effect. But attempts to deal with trade effects without dealing with the underlying supply and consumption effects are most certainly doomed to failure.

The only really measurable limits on subsidies are those on the quantity of product receiving the subsidy. Limits on subsidy expenditures have been suggested, but anyone who has ever run an agricultural subsidy program knows that there are myriad ways to disguise subsidy expenditures. Moreover, changes in exchange rates would further complicate measurements and international comparisons of subsidy expenditures.

On some major issues that are important in agricultural trade, GATT rules are silent. This round of trade negotiations must address two of them: voluntary restraint agreements (VRAs or VERs) and differential import duties or export taxes.

VOLUNTARY RESTRAINT AGREEMENTS

Voluntary restraint agreements generally are the policy tool of large importing countries that deploy substantial hypocrisy to maintain the facade of GATT legality. Under the threat of more drastic action, the exporting country agrees to limit its exports of some product to the market in question. VRAs are generally bilateral in nature and can be highly disruptive to both the supplying country and to third-country suppliers because of the diversion effects on trade.

At a minimum, rules ought to be developed regarding compensation for accepting VRAs that reduce export earnings, and interested third parties should have an opportunity to review such agreements. At present, such arrangements do not require compensation, are not subject to GATT review and, despite their significant effects, allow powerful importers to apply import restrictions without significant economic and political costs. Since these arrangements presumably provide substantial economic and political benefits to the protected groups in importing countries, it seems unreasonable to have all the costs borne by others. Therefore, a system should be developed for more evenly distributing the costs and benefits. Without such rules, the VRA approach to agricultural trade will almost certainly be used more widely. To the extent that other forms of import restrictions are made more difficult because of changes in rules resulting from these negotiations, the incentives to use VRAs will rise even further.

DIFFERENTIAL TAXES AND TARIFFS

Developing countries have complained for decades about the developed countries' pervasive use of differential tariffs, which increase as the level of processing increases, to protect domestic processing industries. It is true that this practice is common and that it does distort trade by reducing the ability of raw material producers to export processed products.

In recent years, a number of developing countries have used differential export taxes to reduce incentives to export unprocessed products, the most visible case being oilseeds and vegetable oils. Malaysia, Argentina, and Brazil, until recently, applied higher export taxes on unprocessed oilseed products than on processed products (oil and meal). Oilseed processors in both the EC and the United States have filed trade cases with their respective governments charging unfair trading practices. In fact, the most seriously injured parties are the raw product producers in the exporting countries whose prices are depressed.

There thus seem to be grounds for a negotiation whereby both sides would gain. Negotiations would involve agreement among developed countries to equalize their tariffs on all stages of processed products in return for agreement with the developing countries to equalize their export taxes on the same basis. Investment in processing industries could be made much more rationally in both sets of countries with these changes. The present systems tend to encourage overinvestment in both situations.

Organizing Negotiations

Subsidies and import barriers do not exist in an abstract form; they apply to specific products. Different specific products are of great interest to some countries and of little interest to others. On the other hand, several of the various types of devices are used to protect agriculture in almost every country.

Negotiations can be organized in two ways and the organization can significantly affect their outcome. Traditionally, trade negotiations in agriculture have been organized by commodity groupings—for example, grains, oilseeds and oilseed products, bovine meat, dairy products, fruits and vegetables. The strong tendency, in terms of both tradition and interest, will be to continue this approach.

A better approach would be to start by dealing first with the general issues of rules to be applied to various types of import controls and subsidies, leaving the issue of applying principles to specific commodity situations until the end. There are sound reasons for using this approach.

Attaining consistency and compatibility is a major problem when dealing with policies, as this negotiation is supposed to. Within nearly every country there is great mobility of agricultural resources over a wide range of products. There is a universal tendency to try to deal with a commodity, only to find that in doing so the problem is pushed into another commodity. Dealing with policy instruments first and consistently, and then dealing with specific commodities, is one way of avoiding this problem.

Recent history is full of examples of national policies that have had major unintended side effects upon other commodities and other countries. In the United States the Food Security Act of 1985 mandated a whole-herd dairy buy-out program. It was designed to reduce dairy surpluses by paying farmers to cease dairy production. Participating dairy farmers had to either export their dairy cattle or sell them for slaughter and agree not to reenter dairy production for some years in the future. Since beef producers were worried, the government undertook to buy 200 million pounds of beef in the market, half of which had to be exported.

The program worked insofar as dairy production was concerned. But the fall in live cattle prices was much greater than anticipated despite the government purchases. Thus, beef cattle producers complained bitterly about the effect of the program on them. The USDA bought the beef as required and sold a significant amount of it to Brazil at a fraction of its cost. This, of course, hurt other beef exporters, especially the Argentines and Australians. Thus, what started as a simple program to reduce domestic dairy price support costs resulted in substantial effects upon both domestic and foreign beef producers.

The EC dairy production controls imposed in 1984 had some of the same side effects, complicated by the intervention mechanism for beef and grains. So, while the program reduced dairy support costs, it almost certainly increased beef and grain support costs by increasing the supply of bovine meat and reducing the demand for feed. This, in turn, put pressure on the EC to increase exports of beef and grains, thereby affecting other exporters.

These are two examples of the way in which domestic policy changes made to deal with one commodity problem affect the markets for other commodities worldwide. They illustrate how difficult it is to adjust policy and the importance of multilateral, rather than unilateral, action. It is important that these negotiations not result in solving problems in one commodity by creating problems in others.

A second reason for dealing with policy issues and not commodities is that different countries have different economic and political interests in individual commodities. There is a major danger in these negotiations that two or three of the dominant traders in a given commodity will strike a deal that will serve their interests without regarding the effects either on smaller countries or on other commodities.

The greatest danger in these negotiations is that the two most powerful participants in the negotiations, the EC and the United States, will reach accommodations that meet their most pressing political needs without dealing with the basic issues. Each of them might, in turn, strike a bilateral arrangement with Japan on a few specific items.

Political pressures by the major powers will be immense in driving the negotiations in this direction. Japan has always found it easier politically to negotiate individual, bilateral, commodity-by-commodity arrangements than to make across-the-board changes in import barriers. The new negotiations will put similar pressures on the United States and the EC by encouraging agreements that disturb domestic programs as little as possible.

Commodity Issues and Country Interests

Farmers in different countries produce commodities and tend to view what happens to these specific commodities as the major determinant of their well-being. Trade takes place in the form of commodities, and specific policies regarding the imports and exports of commodities are what trade policy is about. Thus, sooner or later, these trade negotiations, like all others, must come to commodities.

Of course, the negotiations actually are about resource use and what the returns to resources will be in different countries. But that is too abstract to be dealt with in a trade negotiation, and therefore the issue of resource use will be dealt with by negotiating rules relating to trade in commodities. Thus, it eventually will be necessary to develop specific rules for each of the major commodity groups discussed in chapter 3, and for some others, such as fruits and vegetables, and wines, where market intervention devices generally are different.

7 Policy Recommendations

Even a brief review shows that agricultural policies in most countries are in disarray and no longer fit world economic and political conditions. At this point, it is useless and even counterproductive to point at any one system or any one country. The fault lies with thousands of past decisions, both public and private, based upon incorrect assumptions as to how the world would be in the 1980s and beyond. These decisions were made with good intentions and, for the most part, good purposes. They have led, however, to an intolerable situation that must be addressed.

The time has arrived for fundamental decisions to be made by the member countries of the General Agreement on Tariffs and Trade (GATT) concerning both the rules for international trade in agriculture and the nature of their domestic agricultural support systems. The two decisions are bound together. It is not possible to have free domestic agricultural markets and government-controlled and managed international markets. Conversely, it is not possible to have free international markets for agricultural products and tightly controlled and managed domestic markets. In the modern world, domestic and international markets are intricately interlinked, and the ability of a single country or trading bloc to separate them is limited.

Policymakers and agricultural producers must face some unpleasant realities. One is that the long-run downward trend of real agricultural commodity prices will likely continue. This trend is the result of a continuing stream of cost-reducing agricultural technologies that improves the conversion of sunlight, air, and water into edible products, either directly or indirectly. This technology cannot be stopped, nor should it be, for economic progress is measured by the ability of mankind to meet basic human needs for food, clothing, and shelter with fewer resources and less human energy. In fact, some observers of the new biotechnology are predicting that the pace of the technological change will increase. If they are correct, the decline in real prices will accelerate and the pressures on policies that attempt to maintain prices will increase. Increased productivity coupled with a relatively slow

133

growth in demand means declining real prices. This phenomenon has been true in the past and will be in the future as well.

Second, there is no reason to assume that agricultural producers should and will be permanent wards of the state in industrial market economies or that they should be immune to market forces. Many countries have developed programs to protect farmers, generally at great cost to their consumers and treasuries. It is doubtful, however, that consumers and policymakers intended or expected these programs to become permanent sources of income, totally unrelated to market demand for the products produced.

Third, despite the current large expenditures on farm subsidies, the agricultural sectors do not dominate most developed countries. Sooner or later the overall political and economic interests of those economies will prevail. The high cost of agricultural programs is already a major source of concern in many countries as pressures mount to reduce public spending.

However, it has taken years, and in some cases decades, to arrive at the present economic difficulties, and it is unrealistic to assume that they can be easily and quickly dealt with. Both a change in direction and an agreement as to where the process will lead are needed.

Objectives of the Negotiations

If policymakers are to deal effectively with the current situation, the negotiations must be truly comprehensive. The ultimate objective, of course, was laid out in the ministerial declaration: "Negotiations shall aim to achieve greater liberalization of trade in agriculture and bring all measures affecting import access and export competition under strengthened and more effective GATT rules and disciplines."

However, to paraphrase the old joke about asking directions to a certain place from a native—"You can't get there from here"—in order to reach the ultimate objective, it will be necessary to have some interim objectives that are consistent with and contribute to the final objective. Those interim objectives must be:

● an agreement that brings about sufficient production constraints and consumption increases to end stock building

● an agreement regarding the disposal of the excessive stocks of grains, dairy products, and beef

● a "cease-fire" in the steadily escalating subsidy war.

Anyone who believes in achieving the major objective of the negotiations—liberalizing trade by improving market access, increasing discipline on the use of subsidies, and reducing the negative effects of subsidies on trade—will immediately protest that dealing with current market problems is likely to involve more, rather than less, government intervention and is, therefore, inconsistent with the final objective. However, government actions in part got us where we are today, and it is inconceivable that some of the current problems can be handled without government action to offset the sudden and large declines in commodity prices and producers' incomes that would occur if all the corrections were left to market forces. It is important that the interim measures do not become permanent measures, for if they do, the system will evolve slowly into a completely managed system.

FREEZING SUBSIDIES

The freeze or standstill on agricultural subsidies should be comprehensive in terms of commodity coverage and should include all nations participating in the negotiations.

The freeze should be agreed and implemented without prejudging any future negotiations concerning the status of specific subsidies and their limits. Countries should not gain or lose negotiating position by freezing their subsidy programs. On the surface, the idea of freezing subsidies appears simple but, as is always the case, the implementation will be much more complex. The issues that need to be decided include what is to be frozen and what constitutes a freeze.

The subsidies included in such a freeze ought to be all measures that affect supply and demand for agricultural commodities in the individual countries and in world trade. The most obvious starting point is producer prices or consumer prices, or both. If a country has a program that uses import controls to achieve a desired level of producer prices, a freeze would mean that the prices received by producers would not be increased by the use of quotas, intervention mechanisms, or other devices. The same would be true of target prices achieved by the use of direct deficiency payments. A freeze on consumer prices is only relevant where consumer prices are fixed or influenced by a government agricultural program.

One approach that has been suggested is to freeze levels of protection as measured by the producer subsidy equivalents (PSEs) used in OECD studies. This approach is not the best for several reasons. The USDA sums up the difficulties in a recent analysis: "Changes in PSE's and CSE's can be due to country policy changes, or changes in world reference prices, or exchange rates. These measures can be quite variable over time."[1] Farmers, however, respond to prices received in their own currencies and to their own production costs. It is farmers' incentives that need to be dealt with and PSEs may or may not do this. Therefore, what should be frozen is the absolute or maximum price in the local currency where that price is a function of a subsidy or protection program.

Any freeze should contain two elements: a freeze on the unit value of the subsidy and a freeze on the quantity subsidized. Unless both elements are covered, a subsidy freeze will not have the intended effect, i.e., to stop further expansions in output in response to the subsidy or protection program.

Similar criteria should be applied to export subsidy programs of all types. The subsidy per unit should be frozen as well as the number of units that are subsidized.[2] This freeze should extend to direct export subsidies, export-credit subsidies, transportation subsidies, and deficiency payments on exports.

In the case of the US grains program, for instance, this freezing strategy would involve freezing the target prices, the quantity upon which target prices are paid, direct export subsidies in terms of both volume covered and quantity per unit, and interest-rate subsidies on export credits. In the case of the EC, it would involve capping the target and intervention prices, capping the variable levies, and limiting both the amount of export restitutions (to levels no greater than the base period) and the volume upon which restitution is paid.

The freeze should also include a freeze on the levels of prices paid to producers by state buying agencies and/or on the levels of resale prices charged to consumers by those same agencies *where the prices involved are above world prices*. At the same time, the margin of difference between the internal buying price and the export price should be capped where state trading is used for exports.

It also is important that access to markets protected by quotas, VERs, and other import restrictions be frozen at not less than existing levels at the same

---

1. USDA Economic Research Service, *Government Intervention in Agriculture*, Foreign Agricultural Economic Report No. 229, April 1987, p. 21.
2. Some allowance or adjustment would need to be made for changes in the exchange rates. No adjustments should be allowed for changes in world prices, however, or the freeze would merely be a quantity freeze.

time. In the absence of a freeze on minimum access, importing countries that use restrictions to protect domestic producers would gain an advantage over exporting countries.

The freezing of subsidies resulting from the use of import quotas is simple in concept, but more difficult in practice. The goal should be the same, i.e., that the controls be operated so that the domestic price to producers does not rise, and the quantity of domestic output receiving the high guaranteed price does not increase. Administering the price limit is not difficult, but the quantity limitation is difficult.

There are several ways to achieve the quantity limitation; the effectiveness and feasibility depend upon the product. One way to reach a rough equivalent is to guarantee specific access in terms of a quantity, but this automatically guarantees the market growth to the subsidized domestic producers unless a market-growth factor is included. Another method of limiting benefits would be to assess a levy on domestic producers for any output above their output in the base period. The levy should amount to the difference between the high domestic price under the import quotas and the world price of the product. This method could be used for sugar, dairy products, and other goods that farmers sell directly to processing plants. It would be difficult to apply to grains used on farms for feed or to livestock sales. However, civil servants and producers' organizations which have been so inventive in developing subsidies certainly can, with the same inventiveness, develop ways to limit them effectively.

It is important to remember what the freeze is intended to do and not to do. It is not intended to limit output. Any producer in any country who can profitably expand output in the absence of subsidies should be allowed to do so. The freeze is not intended to limit exports; it is intended only to limit the exports receiving subsidies of any kind.

The freeze is not intended to raise commodity prices, although it might because of the important effect it could have on expectations about the future. It is merely meant to stop the further depression of world commodity prices by expanding subsidized output.

The standstill will require the choice of a base period. It should be a recent base period, even though that period contains record levels of protection and subsidies for producers in most countries. Attempting to freeze subsidies at levels of some past period becomes unduly complicated and would be more difficult politically. In the case of crops, the standstill should apply to the first harvest after the agreement is reached. For dairy, poultry, and livestock products, where production is continuous, the subsidy freeze should begin on a predetermined calendar date.

The measures to be frozen and the methods that each country will use to implement the freeze should be provided by the individual country. Each country should provide a list of measures important enough to be included, the levels of prices at which the freeze will occur, and the physical quantities of products covered by the existing programs. These lists of programs, prices, and quantities would, of course, be subject to review by the monitoring group and challenge by other countries; but the standstill should not be a negotiation over what future programs should be.

Two important elements need to be included in a standstill agreement. One is the establishment of a monitoring group to monitor the progress of a freeze. This group could provide a useful function both in the monitoring of a standstill and in subsequent monitoring of follow-up actions taken in response to the negotiations.

The second issue that needs to be related to a standstill in agricultural subsidies is a fixed, agreed-upon timetable for completing the negotiations. In the absence of such a timetable, there will be a tendency for some nations to delay, which in turn will increase the frustration and likelihood that other nations will react with more adverse trade actions.

The current trade negotiations must show progress, a need greater in agriculture than in almost any other field of trade. While progress in agriculture cannot guarantee progress elsewhere, the absence of progress in agriculture might cause a major breakdown in the entire multilateral trade negotiations (MTN) process. Freezing subsidies would mark some real progress and could realistically be presented as the "early harvest" some have promised.

Dealing with Distortions in Agricultural Trade

The heart of the GATT negotiations for agriculture lies in intentions to "reduce import barriers" and "reduce the adverse impact of subsidies on agricultural trade."

It is important for negotiators and various agricultural groups in their respective countries to have a clear vision of what the negotiations are about and what they are not about. The negotiations are not addressing how much income is transferred to the farm sector in individual countries. If countries choose or feel compelled to make large income transfers to their farm populations, it is their prerogative to do so.

The negotiations will attempt to devise rules that will remove or reduce the adverse effects on trade of governmental measures designed to transfer income to farmers. In the ideal world, the need for such government programs would disappear, but in the real world this is unlikely to happen any time soon.

Another important task in the negotiations will be to devise rules that will provide a smooth transition from where we are now to where we want to end up. Given the magnitude and complexity of present programs, this is important because the transition period should probably be fairly long and, unless the rules for transition are spelled out clearly, there will be an infinite possibility for problems and misunderstandings.

Participants should enter the process with some of the positive elements in mind. If the actions are taken on a broad multilateral basis, the adjustments for the producers in any one country will be far less than would occur under unilateral reform or bilateral agreements.

It should be noted that for almost all agricultural products, the equilibrium price is certain to be higher rather than lower than current world prices if the present subsidy-induced distortions are removed. Estimates of market equilibrium made using the programs of the early 1980s suggested the distortions were significant and that commodity prices would rise between 10 percent and 20 percent.[3] By 1986 the market distortions were much greater, probably amounting to between 30 percent and 40 percent in grains and even more in dairy products.[4] Therefore, gradual reduction or removal of government subsidies would not have the massive depressing effect on farm prices in most countries that some people might expect.

This does not mean that there would not be major adjustments involved for farm producers in many countries. All of the estimates of long-run price effects of trade liberalization assume that production adjustments occur that remove high-cost producers from production. Thus, as we saw in tables 4.5, 4.6, and 4.7, there would be major declines in producer welfare in some countries and for high-cost producers in most countries.

---

3. Rodney Tyers and Kym Anderson, "Distortions in World Food Markets: A Quantitative Assessment" (a background paper for *World Development Report 1986*, World Bank Washington).
4. World market prices for agricultural products have fallen sharply since 1980–82. See table 2.2.

The Approach to Negotiations

Three alternative approaches can be taken in the negotiations on import barriers and agricultural subsidies:

• a system that phases out all import controls and domestic agricultural subsidies that affect international trade

• a system that develops a completely managed trade system for agriculture similar to the one embodied in the Multi-Fiber Arrangement for international textile trade

• a system that allows diversity in national agricultural programs as long as those programs do not adversly affect international trade.

Each of these approaches has appeal, and each has political and economic pitfalls.

MOVING TO A SYSTEM WITHOUT DISTORTIONS

The simplest and most intellectually satisfying approach would be to get an agreement whereby all countries would agree to phase out all forms of import controls and all subsidies—domestic and export—which affect international trade. This would also imply that all state trading that maintains internal prices different from world prices would be abolished.

This is the essence of the proposal by the Reagan administration, presented in Geneva on July 6, 1987. The United States proposed that all programs, including public research and extension, be reduced to zero over a 10-year period. It suggested that the producer subsidy equivalent (PSE), developed by the Organization for Economic Cooperation and Development (OECD) in its study of agricultural subsidies, be used as a measure of subsidy levels and to monitor progress in phasing out subsidy programs.

This approach would leave open only which of the various import controls and subsidies should be dealt with in this fashion and the time period in which they would be phased out. If governments find it necessary to provide income to their farmers beyond what they receive from world market prices, governments still would be able to make income transfer payments unrelated to agricultural production. This, of course, is called "decoupling" and is especially popular with economists.

This approach to dealing with agricultural programs implies that all such programs should be phased out so that over time the agricultural industry remaining in a country would be determined by its ability to compete in world markets. Production and consumption decisions and trade in agricultural products would be free from interference from government intervention.

Even though this approach would be the simplest, it is unlikely to be acceptable to farm producer groups in many countries. Producers in a number of countries know they would not be competitive in world markets. In some other cases, being competitive would require a substantial decline in land prices, which present landowners would oppose.

Even if the existing farm producers were to be compensated fully by direct government income transfers not tied to production, many people would object to phasing out farm production in those that would be affected. They would cite local employment and development issues, environmental issues, and minimum food security. Providers of farm inputs, agricultural marketing and processing firms dependent upon these production areas, also have a vested interest in keeping these producers in place and in production.

The argument that governments could continue to make income transfers to farmers unrelated to their agricultural production is not likely to persuade most farm groups to give up their present income transfer programs. Producer groups in most countries will not be pleased to have the full extent of the income transfers involved in the programs made explicit by shifting these transfers entirely to the public treasuries. They feel, probably correctly, that the public tolerance for large income transfers to individual producers would be limited, and that such transfers would be limited to smaller producers by some sort of means test.

The kind of adjustment suggested by this approach could be made more easily by the United States than by Japan or the EC. This is because the United States already uses direct government payments as the major way of supporting producer income, whereas the EC and Japan use broader measures that achieve the income transfers largely through higher consumer prices. For wheat, for instance, the budget only contributes 31 percent of the income transfer in the EC, 33 percent in Japan, and 100 percent in the United States.[5] Even in the United States this approach has been rejected by the sugar producers and is viewed with skepticism by many other agricultural groups.

Public officials who run these agricultural programs in many countries also

---

5. USDA Economic Research Service, *Government Intervention*, table 8, p. 34.

know that income transfers under present programs are much larger than public expenditures and that obtaining enough public funds to replace the present programs completely would be impossible. This would be especially true in the EC and Japan. The success of this approach will finally depend upon the ability of the potential "winners" under a free market system to overcome the political opposition from the potential "losers" in their own country and in other countries.

Domestic political realities in a number of key players, including the United States, Japan, and the EC, appear to preclude true trade liberalization in agriculture by phasing out most or all domestic agricultural programs. During this period of substantial overcapacity, declining world prices, and declining incomes, agricultural producers will be most reluctant to give up known programs for uncertain market prices. Individual countries may, for their own internal political reasons, decide to phase out completely their various programs of agricultural protection. For some commodities, a significant number of countries must be able to make commitments to end all government programs. In these cases, the countries concerned should get full credit for such efforts whatever their motivation.

MOVING TO MANAGED TRADE

In every agricultural trade negotiation, substantial interest in developing a system of managed world trade is usually manifested. In the Kennedy Round of trade negotiations in the 1960s, this took the form of a wheat agreement that attempted to manage both price and quantity trading relations. In the Tokyo Round in the 1970s, a proposal was made to develop commodity agreements for grains, meats, dairy products, and sugar to stabilize prices in world markets. The wheat agreement of the Kennedy Round soon broke down under market pressures. In the Tokyo Round no agreement was ever reached on commodity agreements that attempted to manage international prices.[6]

Despite these past failures, it is almost certain there will be a strong push in the Uruguay Round for some kind of managed market in agricultural products. The arguments for such an approach are persuasive. Almost every country has some kind of internal market intervention for agricultural products.

---

6. An international sugar agreement was negotiated outside the Tokyo Round. It finally collapsed under the world market pressures of the 1980s.

It is politically and economically unrealistic to expect to dismantle these domestic programs. Therefore, it will be argued, international trade rules in agriculture should be adopted to fit the realities of domestic programs.

This approach would deal with market access by negotiating bilateral or multilateral access agreements for specific quantities of specific products. The methods used to control access would be left to each country and its policies. This approach probably would be favored by countries such as Korea and Japan, which have used it extensively, and by some commodity groups in the United States such as sweetener and dairy producers.

This approach would deal with subsidies by allocating or specifying fixed quantities or market shares of world trade for exporting countries having either export subsidies or domestic subsidies that apply to export commodities. This approach would attempt to extend and spell out, commodity by commodity, the equitable share provision of Article XVI:3 of GATT that has proven so troublesome.

This approach is appealing because it is familiar and would not require any major changes in the underlying domestic policies of most major trading nations. Though appealing, this approach is probably unworkable on several counts. First, several of the major trading nations, probably including the United States, Canada, Australia, and Argentina, would find it unacceptable in principle and refuse to participate. Even if this were not the case, such an agreement would most likely be unnegotiable. Would the market share for the United States be the 1980 levels or the 1985 levels? What inducements could be given low-cost producers (such as Thailand for rice) to enter agreements to limit exports? How do you deal with new entrants to export trade, especially if they do not use subsidies?

Finally, this approach would almost certainly prove unworkable even if it were negotiable. The agricultural industry is constantly undergoing major changes in technology that will drastically lower production costs and increase output. Such changes are almost ready in several fields of animal production, including dairy and swine production.

In addition, agricultural output—especially of crops—will vary from year to year as weather and other conditions vary. World agricultural demand will grow (or decline) by unpredictable amounts. Widespread government intervention of the type required to make managed trade work will increase instability in an industry where supply and demand characteristics already make instability a problem. The world is littered with the remains of international commodity agreements that have not worked, including those for wheat, coffee, sugar, and tin. There is no reason to expect that trade agreements to manage agricultural commodity trade will work any better than agreements to manage stocks and prices have in the past.

A FEASIBLE COMPROMISE

Given the significant political and economic barriers that make the move to a completely liberal trading system by abolishing all domestic agricultural programs unlikely, it appears necessary to look for a system that avoids the alternative of a managed trade system. What is needed is a trading system that is applicable to a large number of countries, negotiable abroad, and politically acceptable at home in the countries concerned.

To meet these criteria some general principles need to be followed. Among them are:

● The rules for trade should not attempt to produce a single agricultural system. For many reasons countries will insist on individual systems.

● International prices and trade flows in agriculture should not be frozen, but should be related to world supply and demand factors.

● Farm output should not be increased in response to artificial prices induced by programs designed to protect farm income.

● Increases in farm output necessary to meet increased demand for food should be produced by low-cost producers.

● Programs that seriously distort consumption and production patterns should be altered over time to limit or reduce their distorting effects.

This approach implies that the major efforts in the negotiations should be focused on ways to reduce the adverse trade effects of domestic agricultural programs rather than upon abolishing the programs. Moreover, this approach implies that the consumer-welfare effects of the programs are an internal political issue, not a trade issue. The same is true of a program's internal effects upon resource prices (land). If a country chooses to have agricultural programs that make its agriculture less competitive, it should have the right to do so, *as long as the programs do not expand agricultural output at the expense of other producers.*

In economic terms the following proposals are a second-best approach to reducing the trade difficulties that have typified agricultural rules in the

GATT almost from the beginning. Here are the essential elements of this approach:

● Policies should be altered to ensure that all increases in agricultural output and the inputs used to produce such increases be paid a market return for the increased output.

● Policies should aim to end the payment of all subsidies on products entering international markets. This would include, for example, export subsidies, target-price payments related to output that is exported, and transportation subsidies.

● Special attempts should be made to remove policies that substantially reduce consumption.

● It is neither important nor reasonable to expect that all countries will adopt the same policy systems or that all will move to a free-market system for agriculture. What is important is that all systems operate in a way to achieve the same objectives.

There is a sound economic rationale for these policy recommendations. It is that the most important economic distortions caused by current policies come from the allocation of additional productive resources to agricultural production because producers are receiving more than the market would pay for additional output. Therefore, programs should be changed so that producers receive world market prices for additional output.

A corollary assumption is that many of the resources now engaged in agricultural production and receiving returns inflated by subsidy programs would have little value if they moved into other employment. Thus, the short-run economic gains to be achieved by forcing these resources from agricultural production to other uses are limited because of the age of farmers, immobility of some farm inputs, and lack of alternative opportunities in the nonfarm economy. This implies that sharp reductions in farm prices will not cut farm output much in the short run. The major resource shifts occur when decisions are made to commit new resources to production.

It is also assumed that consumption effects of many programs are not very important because in most developed countries the elasticity of demand for food at the retail level is quite low. Moreover, for most food products, farm prices make up only a fraction of the retail price because much of the consumer price pays for transportation, processing, and marketing of the products.

This means that if farm prices fall, as they would if the various protective measures were removed completely while excess capacity exists, the fall in the retail price would be much less proportionately and the change in consumption would be very small.

To illustrate the point, let us use the example of wheat used to make bread. In the United States, the value of the wheat in a loaf of bread was about 7 percent of the retail price of bread in 1986. Thus, if the farm price of wheat declines 20 percent, this means the retail price of bread might fall 1.4 percent. Assuming that the price elasticity of bread is .10, this implies that consumption would increase an insignificant one-tenth of 1 percent.

Of course, the price elasticities for some products in some countries are significantly higher than for cereals in developed countries. But the elasticities relative to changes in farm prices would be low for most products in developed countries because of the marketing and processing costs associated with products at the consumer level. However, if there is a shift from using prices to using direct payments to transfer income, *priority should be given to products with the higher price elasticities*. In other words, a shift to the use of income payments as a method of transferring income is far more important for meat, dairy, and poultry products than for cereals and sugar.

Thus, MTN objectives should be:

● reducing the effect of subsidies on third-country markets by reducing or ending the production and price distortions in those markets resulting from subsidies

● ending the artificial incentives to increase agriculture output

● guaranteeing some level of access for nonsubsidized producers into markets where prices are maintained above world market levels.

If subsidies were ended in international markets, world market prices would more accurately reflect real costs.

There are a number of reasons for concentrating on the international market distortions. One is that an increasing portion of agricultural products in international trade is imported by developing countries, where both population growth and income elasticities are higher. But most developing countries also have a significant portion of their population engaged in agricultural production. The present price distortions make it difficult, if not impossible, for these countries to have an optimal price policy and resource allocation. Secondly, the major market growth in world trade for agricultural products will be in those countries; who benefits from these growing markets should be determined by production efficiency rather than by whose government spends the most.

The following proposals are based upon the preceding analysis and premises. They do not involve the wholesale abandonment or rewriting of present GATT rules, nor the abandonment of subsidies to agriculture. They do, however, involve some significant changes in the way in which subsidy programs are operated.

Import barriers.   The starting point of the negotiations on import controls must be a decision on Article XI and its exceptions for agriculture. A basic decision is needed on whether to abolish the exceptions completely or to set meaningful limitations on the use of quantitative restrictions. Unless a system to put all quotas under the same strict rules can be agreed upon, the entire concept of import liberalization is meaningless.

Negotiations regarding rules relating to import barriers should aim for these general principles:

● All forms of import barriers should be brought under GATT rules and surveillance.

● The rules should be the same for all countries, i.e., all derogations and grandfather clauses should be removed or phased out.

● Commodities that are close substitutes should be treated in parallel.

As a practical matter, it would be better to have QRs used under uniform rules than under no general rules at all, as is now the case. Therefore, it would appear useful to:

● bring all use of QRs under the same rules, which means ending or phasing out grandfather clauses, the US Section 22 waiver, and similar inconsistencies

● limit their use to situations where meaningful controls over domestic production of the product and all close substitutes exist, as long as the QRs maintain internal prices above world prices

● require minimum access commitments for all QRs so that domestic production cannot displace imports.

State trading.   Several major import barriers are not now subject to GATT discipline (see chapter 4). Most notable are the use of state trading as a method of maintaining import controls, and the use of voluntary export restraints (VERs or VRAs). For a number of countries, the use of state trading is a matter of national systems. In other cases, state trading is used in a food security context, as with rice in Japan. In other cases, as with beef in Japan, the use of state trading is more a matter of administrative convenience than of food security.

The ideal situation would be for countries that use state trading primarily as a price support device to convert their system to a straight system of fixed tariffs. These tariffs would then be subject to negotiation, as are all tariffs.

If for reasons of national security or other domestic policy reasons, it is impossible for countries to phase out state trading, it should be subject to the same rules applied to other quantitative restrictions. Those rules would include domestic production controls and minimum access commitments to be carried out annually when internal prices exceed external prices by some negotiated amount. Moreover, as long as import controls are in place and domestic prices exceed world prices, any future increases in consumption should be included as part of the access agreements. Conversely, any decreases in domestic consumption should not be allowed to reduce minimum access agreements.

Voluntary restraints.   At present, the use of "voluntary" restraint agreements falls outside GATT rules. Unless such arrangements are brought under GATT rules, it is inevitable that these will become a favored control device to escape more difficult rules that should be applied under Article XI, Article XXVIII, or both. These agreements have the same benefits as QRs without requiring the importing country to follow the GATT rules relating to quantitative restraints.

Two different approaches could be followed. One approach, prohibiting such agreements, may not be practical. The other, making the cost of using such agreements equivalent to those applying to QRs, would require all VERs to be formally presented and registered with GATT, certain guidelines to be followed for the allocation of imports, and domestic production controls to be applied in a way that ensures that domestic supplies do not displace imports.

Variable levies.   Another import control that operates as a major method of protection is the variable levy. It is especially disruptive to trade because it usually prevents outside producers from competing in the protected market, regardless of their real competitive position or cost structure.

Users think the variable levy a wonderful protective device. Levies can completely isolate domestic markets from external shifts in supply and demand, from shifts in exchange rates, and from more efficient producers. For the same reasons, outsiders view levies as the most disruptive type of major trade barrier.

Unless some GATT rules can be developed regarding the use of variable levies, the idea of reducing the impact of import controls is a hollow one. The ideal approach would convert all variable levies to fixed tariffs. Even if the agreed tariff rates were relatively high, absolute protection for domestic producers would be ended.

If agreement cannot be reached to phase out all variable levies, the next best approach to limiting their adverse impact would be to put a ceiling on the range of such levies and write rules on their use paralleling the rules on the use of QRs and VERs. These rules should include ways of ensuring that domestic production does not displace imports or lead to exports unrelated to world market prices. It could also include domestic production controls, access guarantees, and limits on export subsidies.

The EC has asserted that its common agricultural policy (CAP) cannot be a subject of negotiation. If that is literally true, there is no prospect of a successful negotiation, for it is unrealistic to believe that an economic bloc as important as the EC can maintain a system that totally isolates its producers and consumers from world markets while the rest of the world liberalizes trade.

Placing an upper limit on the variable levy would not violate the fundamental principles of the CAP; a preference would still exist for community producers. Production-control programs clearly do not violate the CAP, for they are already in use for dairy and sugar and are under consideration for other products. Therefore, what will be at issue in negotiations is not the principle, but the reality of adjusting the CAP to reduce its adverse effects.

Dealing with subsidies.   The issue of subsidies, whether domestic or explicit export subsidies, is as sensitive and difficult as the various forms of import barriers. In many cases, they merely are the other side of the coin.

It is important to remember that these negotiations should proceed after a freeze on all subsidies has occurred. Therefore, any increases in output after this freeze should have other causes than subsidies. What should be done with existing and future subsidies thus remains the only issue for negotiation.

Initially, the issue of which subsidies, domestic or export, adversely affect trade should be considered. In theory, any subsidy that expands output or reduces consumption from levels the market would produce adversely affects trade. In practice, it is not quite that simple.

There are three ways to treat the subsidy issue. One method is to ban subsidies entirely; a second is to allow them, but with relatively precise rules as to what types or levels or both can be used; the third is to not worry about subsidies as such, but try to develop workable rules that prevent adverse trade effects.

The third approach is the present one under GATT, and it has not worked. There is no reason to expect that any conceivable refinement, short of absolute and precise market shares, will make this approach work. Since market sharing also will not work for any period of time, this approach is a recipe for more, rather than less, government interference with trade.

It should be remembered that the real issue is subsidies that distort production, consumption, and trade, not transfer payments to farmers and rural residents. There is an unfortunate tendency to equate the two, which is a matter of practice rather than necessity. If the body politic determines that farmers (or others) are unable to earn enough income in the market, payments may be made to supplement that market income. But these payments do not have to be related to the production of any specific agricultural commodity. The present subsidy programs generally achieve income transfers by increasing the price of the commodities sold. Relating payments and income to commodities, not the income transfer involved, distorts resource use and trade.

There may well be some products and some countries where a conversion can be made from present subsidy systems to direct payments not tied to current production. This could be done fairly easily for products that do not use large amounts of agricultural resources. Sugar would be a candidate for such treatment in the United States and in the EC. Others might include rice in the United States and EC, and peanuts in the United States. The prime criteria could be products for which the resource employment is relatively small, and the trade effects of current programs are obviously large.

First, attention should be focused upon subsidies that directly affect trade via export volumes or prices. These include the target-price payments made by the United States on exported crops, the EC export restitutions, the Canadian transport subsidies, and all export credit subsidies not classified as food aid. All such subsidies should be phased out over a period of time, say 10 years, and replaced, if necessary, with instruments that do not artificially encourage farmers to produce for export by offering them returns on products exported above world market prices.

Since all these kinds of subsidies involve substantial direct government expenditure, they could be converted to income payments without the problems inherent in converting some other protection programs. For instance, under the present US wheat program, the target price for 1987 is $4.38 per bushel, the support price is $2.28. The US government is now paying a deficiency payment of $2.10 per bushel multiplied by the producer's base (allotted acreage times program yield). If US policymakers wish to maintain wheat producers' incomes at some level, deficiency payments would need to be shifted to cover only that portion of production used at home, and the payment on the domestic base would need to be increased. No deficiency payments would be made on output destined for export. Thus, the marginal returns facing producers growing for export would equal the world market price instead of the target price, which is now the case.

The same change could be made for commodities subject to marketing loans in the United States. The marketing loan and deficiency payments would be reduced to cover only the amount consumed domestically. If there is a desire to maintain producers' income, the payment per unit of domestic production could be increased. But no marketing loans or deficiency payments would be made on products entering export markets.

The same principle should be applied to products produced in the EC and other countries now using direct export subsidies. Such a device clearly does not violate the principle of the CAP, which already has a variation of this approach for sugar and dairy products. The EC would only have to convert its present direct outlays for export subsidies into direct payments to producers. These payments would be limited to each producer's base share of domestic use. At the same time, a tax on output that exceeded the base could be used to bring the producer return on excess output down to world market prices. Thus, EC producers would face the same marginal price for output entering world markets as would other producers.

Certain principles should apply in bringing these subsidies under control. First, farm income should not be increased by raising domestic prices to offset the lower prices for export output. Raising domestic prices will adversely affect domestic consumption, thus trade indirectly. Second, the marginal price to producers should reflect world prices for any products where output exceeds domestic consumption. It is not enough merely to add a modest surtax (or co-responsibility levy) on all output, for this only lowers the average price and the marginal price a small amount and thus continues the incentive to produce more than the market will absorb.

The immediate reaction from farm producers and policymakers is likely to be that such a policy is too difficult to administer and too cumbersome.

This is not a persuasive argument from the same people who have generated thousands of pages of regulations on every farm commodity produced in their country. In any event, the simplest program is merely to allow market prices to operate; the next best solution is merely to send checks to farmers. And so it appears simplicity has never been a criterion in the past.

A program to move the pricing of all output in excess of domestic needs at market prices would have to be phased in to allow adjustments to occur. Thus, a period of 10 years might be allowed for a gradual adjustment of output mix and output level that would occur in response to market prices for marginal output.

The mechanics of moving to market prices over a phase-in period should be considered. One approach might be to lower the price on the export output by some percentage each year. This would have to be based upon an estimate of the world price when the adjustments were completed, which is difficult if not impossible. A simpler and more effective approach would be to reduce the volume of output upon which higher-than-market prices (or payments) were based by 10 percent each year. This would subject an increasing portion of world trade to market prices each year, whereas slowly reducing prices would continue the present volume of subsidized products in trade for most of the period.

In the case of US programs, the adjustment would work as follows. At present about one-half of the wheat produced is used domestically. Therefore, over a 10-year period, deficiency payments would be phased out for one-half of US wheat production by reducing the payment *base* for deficiency payments by 5 percent per year. If policymakers wished to maintain producers' incomes, it would be possible to do so by increasing the payment level on the quantity consumed domestically.

In the EC the same principle could be applied by revamping the co-responsibility tax already being used. Instead of applying a modest tax on all output sufficient to pay for losses on exports, however, the tax should be enough to cover all losses on an increasing portion of the exports until the tax on production for export covers all the export losses. This system would be similar to the one now used for sugar.

This approach is likely to be opposed by both sides—the purists who wish to see all subsidies in all countries ended, and the interventionists who want to continue the present situation. The approach is designed to achieve one purpose, to ensure that over time the products moving into export markets from any source are being produced for the world market price. This approach recognizes that the markets in the developed market economies are stagnant—population growth is low, income elasticity is low, and demand for food products is highly inelastic. Future growth in world markets will occur in developing countries, and they should be reserved for unsubsidized competition. If it is necessary to reserve all or most of the domestic market in industrial market economies for domestic producers in order to achieve a working market in the rest of the world, so be it. This distinctly second-best solution is vastly superior to a solution involving modest changes that will not resolve any portion of the present problems.

This approach admittedly has some major problems. One involves the freezing of production patterns within countries (or trading blocs). If present production is used as a starting point, low-cost producers cannot compete effectively for their internal markets because high-cost producers will maintain a market share. However, this is also true under present programs; therefore, in this regard, nothing will be made worse than it is now.

Second, the rights to domestic subsidies will be bid into asset values if they are made transferable with the land. This has happened to US tobacco and peanut programs and several of the Canadian marketing board schemes. This issue can be dealt with by granting the subsidy rights to individuals, rather than farm units. If subsidy rights are made nontransferable, they will disappear over time and could be bought or cashed out. This is an important concept because new entrants to farming should enter the industry with the expectation that they will produce at competitive prices, and they should have the right to buy their productive resources at competitive prices. Unless a change is made, the next generation of agricultural producers will enter the business handicapped by having to pay for subsidy streams devised for previous generations.

Income-support and price-stabilization schemes for agricultural products have been around in one form or another in many countries for nearly a century. However undesirable practical realities might be to some, such programs are not going to disappear entirely as a result of this GATT round. However, just as nations are finding that their domestic monetary and fiscal policies are fully interwoven with their trade policies, they also must recognize that their domestic agricultural policies are also related to trade policies. This recognition alone will represent a major step and a break with the past. It is hoped that the Uruguay Round of GATT negotiations can provide another major step in the improved coordination of agricultural policy and trade policy.

Glossary

Acre/hectare	Units used to measure land area. An acre is an area containing 43,560 square feet. A hectare is a land measurement in metric units containing 10,000 square meters and is equal to 2.47 acres.
Coarse grains	These are grains normally called feed grains in the United States. They include corn, barley, oats, millet, and sorghum.
CAP	This term applies to the common agricultural policy of the European Community and encompasses all of the measures taken relating to agriculture that are operated through the Commission of the European Communities.
CCC	The Commodity Credit Corporation is a US Government corporation empowered to carry out the agricultural programs relating to commodity-price stabilization in the United States.
Countervailing duty	An import duty allowed under GATT to offset the value of a subsidy that results in lower import prices.
Deficiency payments	These are government payments given to agricultural commodity producers to make up the difference between the market price and a predetermined target price.
EC	The European Community is a customs union now made up of 12 countries. The EC-6 consists of Belgium, the Federal Republic of Germany, France, Italy, Luxembourg, and the Netherlands. Denmark, Ireland, and the United Kingdom were added to make the EC-9. Greece joined to make the EC-10, and Portugal and Spain became members in 1986 to make the EC-12.
ECU	This is the European currency unit used under the CAP whose value is equal to that of a fixed basket of member-state currencies.
FAO	The Food and Agriculture Organization of the United Nations is the UN body responsible for most technical agricultural issues, some agricultural development programs, and reports on the world agricultural situation.
HFCS	High fructose corn sweetener is a sweetener produced by refining corn and is a perfect substitute for sugar in many uses.
Marketing board	An organization that uses governmental authority to engage in the marketing of agricultural products. Marketing boards usually are given a total monopoly.
PIK	Payment-in-kind is a program that uses commodities rather than money to pay producer subsidies.

PSE	The producer subsidy equivalent is a concept developed to measure what income would be needed to replace a producer subsidy or protection program if it were removed.
QR	A quantitative restriction used to restrict or control the flow of trade across a border.
SDR	The special drawing right is a monetary unit developed and used by the International Monetary Fund whose value is equal to that of a basket of currencies.
Target price	A predetermined price set as a target, using politically determined criteria.
VAT	The value-added tax is a tax levied on the value added to a product at each stage of manufacture and distribution up to retail sales transactions.
VRA or VER	A quantitative restriction on exports to a specific country that is administered by the exporter.
Variable levy	A border tariff that varies with the world price for the product. Under the CAP, the levy is the difference between the lowest offer price and a predetermined internal price.

Selected Bibliography

Aho, Michael, and Jonathan David Aronson. 1986. *Trade Talks: America Better Listen!* New York, NY: Council on Foreign Relations.

Anandarup, Ray. 1987. "Agricultural Policies in Developing Countries: National and International Aspects." World Bank Discussion Paper No. 14, Development Policy Issues Series.

Anderson, Kym, and Rodney Tyers. 1986. "International Effects of Domestic Agriculture Policies." In *Issues in World Trade Policy: GATT at the Crossroads*, edited by R. H. Snape. London: Macmillan.

Browne, William, and Don Hadwiger, eds. 1986. *World Food Policies: Toward Agricultural Interdependence*. Boulder, Col.: Lynne Rienner Publishers.

Bureau of Agricultural Economics. 1985. *Agricultural Policies in the European Community: Their Origin, Nature and Effects on Production and Trade*. Policy Monograph 2. Canberra: Australian Government Publishing Service.

———. 1985. *Inter-sectoral Effects of the Common Agricultural Policy: Growth, Trade, and Unemployment*. Canberra: Australian Government Publishing Service.

Butler, Sir Richard, and Thomas Saylor. 1986. "Tensions in US-EEC Relations: The Agricultural Issues." Occasional Paper. London: British-North American Committee.

Camps, Miriam, and William Diebold, Jr. 1986. *The New Multilateralism: Can the World Trading System Be Saved?* New York, NY: Council on Foreign Relations.

Castle, E., and K. Hemmi, eds. 1982. *US-Japanese Agricultural Trade Relations*. Washington: Resources for the Future.

Cline, William R., ed. 1983. *Trade Policy in the 1980s*. Washington: Institute for International Economics.

Commission of the European Communities. 1986. *The Agricultural Situation in the Community: Report*. Brussels and Luxembourg.

Congressional Research Service. 1984. "Feeding the World's Population: Developments in the Decade Following the World Food Conference of 1974." Report for the Committee on Foreign Affairs for the US Congress, House of Representatives. Washington: Government Printing Office.

Curry Foundation. 1984. *Agriculture, Stability and Growth: Toward a Cooperative Approach*. New York, NY: Associated Faculty Press.

Dam, Kenneth. 1970. *The GATT: Law and the International Economic Organization*. Chicago: University of Chicago Press.

Food and Agriculture Organization (FAO). 1980. *Agriculture: Toward 2000*. Rome.

———. 1981. *The State of Food and Agriculture*. Rome.

Gardner, B. L., ed. 1986. *US Agricultural Policy: The 1985 Farm Legislation*. Washington: American Enterprise Institute.

General Agreement on Tariffs and Trade (GATT). 1979. *Agreement on Interpretation and Application of Articles VI, XVI and XXIII of the General Agreement on Tariffs and Trade*. Geneva.

———. 1986. *International Trade 1985–86*. Geneva.

———. 1987. *The International Markets for Meat—1987*. Geneva.

Hanrahan, Charles; Penelope Cate; and Donna Vogt. 1984. *Agriculture in the GATT: Toward the Next Round of Multilateral Trade Negotiations*. Washington: Congressional Research Service.

Hufbauer, Gary Clyde, and Jeffrey J. Schott. 1985. *Trading for Growth: The Next Round of Trade Negotiations*. POLICY ANALYSES IN INTERNATIONAL ECONOMICS 11. Washington: Institute for International Economics.

Jackson, John. 1969. *World Trade and the Law of GATT*. Charlottesville, Va.: The Michie Company.

————. 1987. "Anticipating Trade Policy in 1987." *Looking Ahead* (Winter).

Johnson, D. Gale. 1973. *World Agriculture in Disarray*. London: Macmillan.

Johnson, D. Gale; Kenzo Hemmi; and Pierre Lardinois. 1985. *Agriculture Policy and Trade: Adjusting Domestic Programs in an International Framework*. New York, NY: New York University Press.

Josling, T. 1980. *Developed Countries' Agricultural Policies and Developing Countries' Supplies: The Case of Wheat*. Washington: International Food Policy Research Institute.

Miller, Geoff. 1986. *The Political Economy of International Agricultural Policy Reform*. Canberra: Australian Government Publishing Service.

Paarlberg, Robert L. 1985. *Food Trade and Foreign Policy: India, the Soviet Union and the United States*. Ithaca, NY: Cornell University Press.

————. 1986. *United States Agriculture and the Developing World: Partners or Competitors?* Washington: Curry Foundation.

————. 1987 (forthcoming). *Fixing Farm Trade: Policy Options for the United States*. A Council on Foreign Relations Book. Cambridge, Mass.: Ballinger Company.

Parikh, Kirit S., and Wonter Tims. 1986. *From Hunger Amidst Abundance Without Hunger*. Laxenburg, Austria: International Institute for Applied Systems Analysis.

Sanderson, Fred. 1987 (forthcoming). *Agricultural Trade Issues*. Washington: Council on US and International Trade Policy.

Schuh, G. Edward. 1985. "Improving US Agricultural Trade." In *The Dilemmas of Choice*, edited by Kent A. Price. Washington: Resources for the Future.

US Department of Agriculture. 1983. *EC Grains, Oilseeds and Livestock: Selected Statistics, 1960–80*. Washington: Economic Research Service.

————. 1986. *Dairy, Livestock and Poultry*. Washington, September.

————. 1986. *Foreign Agricultural Circular*. "World Grain Situation and Outlook." Washington, August.

————. 1986. *World Agriculture Situation and Outlook Report*. Washington, December.

————. 1987. *World Cotton Situation*. Washington, March.

————. 1987. *Foreign Agricultural Circular*. "World Grain Situation and Outlook." Washington, June.

US International Trade Commission. 1985. "Review of the Effectiveness of Trade Dispute Settlement Under GATT and the Tokyo Round Agreements." Report to the Committee on Finance, US Congress, Senate, December.

Valdes, Alberto, and J. Zietz. 1980. *Agricultural Protection in OECD Countries: Its Cost to Less Developed Countries*. Washington: International Food Policy Research Institute.

White, T. Kelly, and C. Hanrahan, eds. 1986. *Consortium on Trade Research and Agriculture: A Comparative Look at US, Canadian, and the EC Policies*. Washington: USDA, Economic Research Service.

White, T. Kelly; Gene Mathia; and C. Edward Overton. 1987. "Global Trends in Agricultural Production and Trade Policy." In *US Agriculture and Third World Development: The Critical Linkage*, edited by Randall Purcell and Elizabeth Morrison. Washington: Curry Foundation.

World Bank. 1982. *World Development Report 1982*. New York, NY: Oxford University Press.

————. 1986. *World Development Report 1986*. New York, NY: Oxford University Press.

SPECIAL REPORTS

FORTHCOMING